More Praise for Alanna Fero and *Love Made Visible*

"Alanna Fero *gets it.* **A modern thought leader on career and work has finally emerged. Bravo!!** At a time when more and more people are questioning the career paths they have chosen, this book presents real possibilities for the change and satisfaction we're all looking for. Fero's writing style is modern and her message is clear: You can make a change and you can do it now. If you're serious about a career move, buy this book. Do as I did – read it, then read it again."

– Christopher Ian Bennett,
Leader, Green Party of British Columbia

"Fasten your seatbelt... the excitement is about to begin... once you pick it up, you won't be able to put it down. Storytelling at its best. You will be drawn in by the real life drama of people – like you! – who are on a heartfelt journey of discovery and transformation. **Alanna Fero's unique blend of wisdom, hard-earned knowledge and enthusiasm for life will inspire you and provide practical guidance to follow your dreams.** *Love Made Visible* is a courageous and smart book."

–Maria LeRose,
Award-winning Television Producer
Moderator, The Dalai Lama Vancouver Dialogues

"In the face of ever-increasing expectations and rapid change at work, **it is easy to become deaf to our own inner voice.** *Love Made Visible* **amplifies that voice and reveals its essential role in success that has** *meaning* **to us.** The message is simple but far from simplistic. It is such an engaging read because it is so real. Fero writes with heart and wit as she shares the authentic struggles, fears, decisions, detours, and triumphs of individuals like you and me – all searching for our unique expression of what it means to be fully engaged today. **I strongly recommend this book** for anyone wishing to cultivate that rare combination of professional success and personal fulfillment."

–Russell Hunter,
National Director, Human Performance Institute Canada

"Be prepared for a magic book without the sleight of hand. **An important and beautiful perspective on what life's work can really be all about** – full, rich and meaningful."

– Jonni O'Connor, PhD,
author of *Living the Energy*

"Alanna Fero has combined two irresistible ingredients for the reader to savor: **the pure joy of dreaming and the down-to-earth satisfaction of achieving success.** Each case study offers concrete specifics of how people achieved their dreams and a heartfelt perspective on never settling for second best. Alanna is relentless in challenging each client to find what matters most to them, and inspiring readers to do the same. Regardless of where you are in your life, this book will challenge you to rethink it and create something fresh and authentic."

– Lynn Sumida, MSW, co-author of
The Extraordinary Within: Welcoming Change & Unlocking Your True Essence

"*Love Made Visible* is a wonderful book for those who know they want more from work and life. Filled with rich stories of those who have found themselves at a turning point, **Alanna's approach... is a great support to deep, authentic transformation.** The book offers a critical tool for building sustained business and personal success by getting us to clarify what we really find important."

– Lynn Corrigan, CHRP,
Regional Human Resources Manager,
Capers Community Markets

"*Love Made Visible* is hard to put down. It's great non-fiction that reads like a gripping novel, keeping you up late at night to get just a few more pages in. I've been a client of Alanna's for several years now – several very good years for me and my business. If you can work with her, you should. She is inspiring and you will never feel more passionate about your life! If you can't, this book is the next best thing. It has her voice and her heart. **Engaging, insightful, and so rich with possibilities, speaking directly to you. I loved it! Read this, then call her.**"

–Diana Zitko, CEO,
Meridian Westcoast Mortgages and
Number One Broker in Western Canada four years running

"*Love Made Visible* is a true delight filled with thought provoking revelations that are constantly challenging and nurturing the reader. **Alanna Fero has beautifully painted each letter in this book with love and devotion.**"

–Andy Chu, CEO,
Arc 2 Entertainment

"When I first met Alanna, I thought maybe she could help me with my resume and increasing my salary and responsibility. I soon discovered, Alanna has a habit of giving you more than you were expecting. A lot more. She helped me recognize my strengths and taught me how they contributed to the corporate bottom line, helping me garner a 30% increase in pay. The best part of it all is now I know I deserve that pay! As I evolve on my career path, Alanna's contribution continues. I am learning how to integrate my values more completely with my career with the end result being a more satisfied and more complete me! **It is so fitting that her new work is called** *Love Made Visible* **– it describes her heart and the experience of working with her perfectly.**"

–Liz van Warmerdam,
Hydrogeologist

"Working with Alanna, having her hear me and embrace my dream as only she can, has brought me to very happy tears. Her passion for my dreams is as great as my own. **Her responses are so warm and sure, it felt like I was receiving my first real hug. And that hug is on these pages.** Read this book and embrace your possibilities."

–Margherita Porra,
Creative Director, Some Design

"It's great to be working again and I hold the whole experience with a lightness I never had before. My boss is already talking long term and wants to make me Chief Operations Officer – to which I responded (you would have been proud!) Balance! Family! Four day work week! and he accepted. This new beginning feels like a total rebirth. **Thank you, Alanna. For being a light in the dark forest, guiding me back to my path.** For helping me rediscover my abilities and aspirations. For helping me to believe again - in myself, in possibility... I'm so thankful that I reached out to you and so grateful that the hand you offered me was such a true and generous one. The right one. I've begun holding you in my mind as the Glynnis the Good Witch from The Wizard of Oz – helping people get home. Here's hoping you help many more."

– J. Powell, COO

"*Love Made Visible* positively compels readers to imagine their own most worthy life, and to trust the creative and often erratic journey that brings it into being. Alanna Fero writes an engaging narrative; a stream of fresh air, each chapter a mystery novel tracking the roller coaster of Big Transition in work and life. Real life stories that glow with permission, credibility, honesty and enthusiasm. **A transparent and generous guide, Alanna's support and "no-holds-barred" wisdom are palpable on every page.** *Love Made Visible* is a great read."

— Oriane Lee Johnston,
Leadership Consultant & Former Program Director, Hollyhock Retreat Centre

"I've worked with Alanna... both as a one-on-one coaching client and a workshop participant. **She attracts clients who are passionate and principled, triple bottom line thinkers and community builders, leaders in the true sense of the word...** Alanna has made her business a true extension of who she is. That's pretty much the highest praise I can think of."

— Grace Tom,
Conference Planner

"In my search for a 'balanced life' I was lucky enough to attend one of Alanna Fero's VIP coaching programs through the Vancouver School Board and then went on to join her famed Encompass "MomenTeam." Alanna nipped in the bud what years of corporate workshops and personal development books failed to do. I have become unstuck and am now experiencing growth and change in my personal and professional life. **Alanna is extremely insightful; her thought-provoking questions have provided significant breakthroughs for me, while at the same time 'squashing' my self-defeatest patterns.** It has been over a year since my last class with Alanna, but I am not finished with her yet. As they say, life is a journey, not a destination, and I plan to check in with Alanna again next year to plan out the next 5-10 years of my 'balanced life'. Thanks to Alanna, I have a renewed sense of purpose!"

— Carol Hannah, Legal Secretary

"Alanna covered a lot of territory in a short time in our workshop series. From visioning and planning to healthy conflict resolution and motivating others, Alanna delivered concrete guidance. She planted the seeds and we'll nurture them to grow. **Alanna's vibrant personality and ability to keep us on track with our objectives made our work totally worthwhile.** She made us think and *act.*"

— Bonnie Clogg, Web Designer

Love Made Visible

Values-Driven Approaches to Work/Life

Alanna Fero

National Library of Canada Cataloguing in Publication Data
www.collectionscanada.ca/amicus/index-e.html

Fero, Alanna Carlene, 1967-

ISBN: 978-1-4251-3587-4

Order this book online at www.trafford.com/07-1400

1. Career   2. Self Help   3. Business/Leadership   I. Title

Printed by Trafford Publishing, Victoria, BC, Canada

Cover and manuscript design by Margherita Porra, Some Design

Cover and inside photos of author by Rob Daly

 www.trafford.com

North America & international
toll-free: 1 888 232 4444 (USA & Canada)
phone: 250 383 6864 ♦ fax: 250 383 6804 ♦ email: info@trafford.com

The United Kingdom & Europe
phone: +44 (0)1865 722 113 ♦ local rate: 0845 230 9601
facsimile: +44 (0)1865 722 868 ♦ email: info.uk@trafford.com

10 9 8 7 6 5 4 3 2 1

For

Raymond Nicholas Fero (1919 – 1997)

who said:

Find a job you love, and you will never work a day in your life.

(Okay, so Confucius said it first, but my Dad said it to me!)

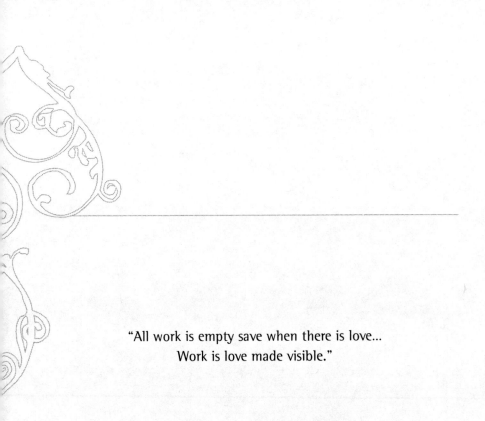

"All work is empty save when there is love...
Work is love made visible."

-Khalil Gibran, *The Prophet*

Table of Contents

Acknowledgements   xvii

Preface   xxv

Introduction   1

Chapter 1
Jump and the Net Will Appear: Moving Your Career Forward
Before You Know Where You Are Going   15

Chapter 2 *Fabulous*
~~Frustrated~~ Artists: Creative Career Paths   35

Chapter 3
Fast Tracks: Type A Overachievers and Work/Life in the C-Suite 51

Chapter 4
Letters After Your Name: Credentialing and Confidence 75

Chapter 5
Making Lemonade
(...When Your Job Is a Lemon But Leaving Isn't an Option) 93

Chapter 6
No Draft Picks, Just Many First Rounds: Life as a Free Agent 111

Chapter 7
Employee to Entrepreneur to Enterprise... Oh My! 131

Chapter 8
Where Everybody Knows Your Name: Workplace Relationships
for Better or for Worse 147

Chaper 9
Blessings in Disguise: Stories of Career Death and Rebirth 167

Afterword 189

About the Author 195

Love Made Visible Keynotes and Workshops 199

Awakening Audacity 201

Love Made Visible

Values-Driven Approaches to Work/Life

Acknowledgements

I've come to know that the manifestation of love that is gratitude is the most powerful emotion I will ever experience, more conducive to moving forward than anything I know – and, happily, gratitude is equally effective in practical or material 'creating abundance' ways as the healing/stretching/ nurturing ways that some of us might more easily expect. Creating dedicated space to give thanks has been a tremendous gift in my life, and guiding my clients to initiate change from a foundation of gratitude for where they are and how far they have already come has brought many breakthroughs. Creating space to give thanks in this manuscript, then, is so much more than the perfunctory recitation of names which typically sandwiches (as briefly as possible) between Contents and content. Gratitude is the centerpiece of this project, the heart from which it grew.

Gratitude itself must be acknowledged.

Thank you to some of my earliest teachers, especially to Catherine Smith, Craig Gillis and Pat Parsons, all of whom expressed compassion and love for my incongruously Type A adolescent self and offered me the gentle wisdom that my life path could be more than my transcript, awards and community service projects, and that filling my heart would serve me so much better in life than filling my head. I can't, of course, say that I heeded their counsel and launched on a very centred and grounded journey right out of high school; in fact, I pretty much brushed them off in my single-minded focus on becoming a high achiever. Yet almost twenty-five years later, I hear their voices more clearly in my writing than I could when I was sitting in their classrooms, and I feel profoundly the gratitude I could not open to at the time.

It reminds me that sometimes 'when the student is ready' and 'the teacher appears,' the learning seed is planted to grow in its own time. When that growth sprouts into willingness, then openness, a lifetime of teachers are within. I can only hope that the people whose lives I have touched with my work take even one snippet away that is as meaningful or lasting as what my lifetime of teachers have given to me.

Thanks also to my grad school mentors, especially Laurie Ricou and Sherrill Grace. Laurie backed me every time my headlong need to 'be myself' got me into hot water with some committee or regulation and his compassion is the primary reason I completed my Master's degree. He was also the first person in my life to tell me I was truly a creative – not just a creative *writer* (though he gave me great confidence in my prose and nudged me toward finding my voice without breaking every rule just for the sake of breaking it...) but actually a creative *live-r*. (And I know he's smiling at my absurd hyphenation, which makes me smile just doing it!) Laurie told me stories of students he had taught over the years who had started as English majors and then gone into corporate work, ROTC, music, the Peace Corps, law school, playwriting, medicine, running bed & breakfasts, and he looked at me and said I was just like them, someone who needed flexibility and stretching, with enough talent and willingness to take risks that I could do anything I wanted. At the time, I only wanted to finish my damn thesis, but I tucked his words away as reserve fuel for the future, and they have served me well.

Sherrill Grace was another warm, welcoming guide who encouraged me to find my own voice. So many professors wanted me to follow in their footsteps; Sherrill encouraged me to walk where I liked. She was brilliant, of course, but just as importantly, she was a beautiful woman who kicked ass in feminist empowerment without giving an inch of her femininity away to do it. Sherrill represented authenticity and options my 21 year-old self needed to see and my 40 year-old self still looks back on with love and thanks.

Thank you to the friends and mentors who generously supported me as I first forayed into teaching and writing, and then into business and career with teaching and writing still holding a place near the centre, especially Karen Boyes, Cherry Davies, Patricia Martin, Leslie Cotter, Kerry Sloan, Erin Soros, Robert Kroetsch, Barry McKinnon, the Langara College English Department, Paul Zollmann and the whole Zollmann family, and the courageous Jennie Wild.

Thank you to my first coaches, Bea Rhodes, Heather Phillips, Lorraine Sims, and the late Thomas Leonard, who mixed tough love and warm hugs to nudge me past my stopping places and into a new world of learning that was holistic and integrated instead of *either* academic *or* experiential. Thanks also to the team at the Human Performance Institute of Canada, especially Marion McAdam and Russell Hunter, who inspired me to make the changes I needed to make to bring *The Power of Full Engagement* to my life and practice, enriching me, my clients and this manuscript.

Thanks to the many people who gave of their time and creativity to make this book a real physical thing and not just something I could see in my head: Margherita Porra for her creative integrity and the beautiful cover and interior design of the manuscript; Rob Daly for the photos which grace this book and my websites; everyone at Trafford for their confident collaboration and willingness to get into the spirit with me of setting my 40th birthday party as the book launch; Alexandra Samuel, Rob Cottingham and the team at Social Signal for the website and blog; Diana Davies and Wendy Lasure for their encouragement during my radio show days; everyone in my BNI networking group over the past six years and especially Maike Engelbrecht, Renee Wilkins and Diana Zitko for inspiring me by the deeply ethical and integrated way they do life/work; the faculty and students at the BCIT BEST program for giving me much-needed structure

Love Made Visible

when I decided to resume a private practice with an entirely new business model; the members of the Centre for Spiritual Living and especially my classmates in CSL's Foundations who showed me every week what it looks like to be the change we seek in the world; Mary Benson for her amazing energy work that helped me want to write again; Susannah Khan and Liz VanWarmerdam for modeling for me the best risk-taking I could ask of a client and then becoming valued friends; Gail Larsen, Joel Solomon, Carol Newell, Lynn Booth and Tim Draimin for supporting me to find my authentic home zone in Real Speaking 2006; Alexandra Parreault for her friendship and so chic styling for photos and television; the incomparable Maria LeRose for her compassionate listening and always true storytelling instincts; and Neale Donald Walsch and the Humanity's Team organizers for one of the best workshops I have ever taken, coming to me by divine appointment at just the right time in the writing to confirm and validate what I had been saying and give me a second wind to sprint to the finish.

Thanks to all the women with whom I have attended the Social Venture Network Women's Gatherings: for the seeds that were planted at Hollyhock and which, gradually and suddenly, took root for me at Asilomar. I could probably write an entire book just about the richness of that experience – this is just a small taste, beginning with my one-on-one time with Cheri Huber, a wise and generous Buddhist teacher whose work I have read voraciously and respected deeply for many years. This momentous opportunity seemed unequivocally like a once-in-a-lifetime thing so I skipped any small talk to go straight to asking her how I could get over my biggest fear. Cheri held my hand as I jumped right over that barrier, so purely and gently that I felt a physical shift in my body, her words and embrace a gift I will treasure as long as I live.

On a roll and just completely *ready* to soak up everything that place and those people had to offer, I was granted some time with women's leadership coach JoAnne Bremm as well. She helped me see that work I'd been possessing as 'my baby' wasn't really mine at all – at best I'd been a good foster mother – and it was time for me to find a way to birth work that really was my own.

The Asilomar evening brought Rhiane Eisler and Phaedra Ellis-Lamkins, women whose work is impactful on a scale beyond which most of us ever dream, let alone achieve. I saw in them the best that I could be and realized that too often I have looked at another's example and used it to feel small by comparison, a waste of the gift they have shared. There is only one way to genuinely honour and accept their gift of inspiration: I must dare to believe that I, too, can be great. Not just to agree with the non-threatening, un-provocative, generally accepted sentiment that there is greatness in all of us and we are all as unique as a snowflake. Nuh-uh. I'm talking about going all the way out on the kind of limb which prompts more than a few people to rev up their chainsaws in anticipation at the thought that someone, let alone a woman, let alone some bred-to-be-modest *Canadian* woman, will crawl out on that shaky branch and audaciously utter the words:

"I have something to say that I want the world to hear."

Thanks to Deb Nelson for organizing the Asilomar event; the dazzling and erudite Cara (wanting to make new scripts, new models for the whole of the life experience we're trying to create); Gail (with The *Velvetine Rabbit* quote that brought me to tears); Barbara (who was the first to hear my quadruple bottom line idea and say 'you have to do it!'); and the amazing Adrienne who got lost with me on the California highways by engrossing me in such engaging conversation that I couldn't possibly think about looking for road signs – thanks to all of them, I was already way out on that branch. I can happily say I live out on that limb now, and so far there have been no chain saws in sight.

Thanks also to the gentle and intuitive Oriane Lee Johnston and the inspiring 'Team Hollyhock' cohort of Diane, Paul, Pat, Lynn, Esther, Sharon, Caroline, Robin and Deidre, holding creative and sacred space for writing, speaking and manifesting.

Thank you to the thousands of individual and corporate clients, workshop participants, radio listeners and tv viewers who have shared their lives and light with me over the years, and given me the gift of service through you. I have received so much more than I ever imagined simply by being present for your experiences, offering the best I can, and trusting that our combined wisdom will elevate us both. Thank you for awakening your audacity, seeking and finding your purpose and passion, letting me companion you on your journey, and sending me postcards from wherever life takes you. Your good news is always the most delicious part!

And the last thank yous are for two incredible women of grace and heart who until recently didn't even particularly know what this book is about, who for a long time only peripherally knew I'd been writing one, but whose blessed guidance came into my life just as I was 'in transition,' the intense final stages of labour in bringing this work into the world, and whose light made the re-visions the easiest and most personally transforming pages for me to write: Mary Kay Ducey and Jonni O'Connor. Thanks for getting me to the tipping point where I can not just quote but now actually live Marianne Williamson's beautiful words from *A Return to Love:*

> Our deepest fear is not that we are inadequate. Our deepest fear is that we are powerful beyond measure. It is our light, not our darkness, that most frightens us. We ask ourselves, who am I to be brilliant, gorgeous, talented, fabulous? Actually, who are you not to be? You are a child of God. Your playing small doesn't serve the world. There is nothing enlightened about shrinking so that other people won't feel insecure around you. We are born to make manifest the glory of God that is within us. It's not just in some of us – it is in everyone. As we let our light shine, we unconsciously give other people permission to do the same. As we are liberated from our own fear, our presence automatically liberates others.

I acknowledge you all with deepest
gratitude and abundant love,

Preface

"You work that you may keep pace with the earth
and the soul of the earth."

- Kahlil Gibran, The Prophet[§]

Work is just play that you get paid for: a belief that is one of my driving values. It should be fun, natural, graceful and even easy – yes, *easy*. If that offends some of your sensibilities about work ethic, professionalism, dedication and commitment, please don't let it. The most devoted workers, the people who put in the longest hours and often achieve some of the highest results and enjoy the most satisfying rewards, are doing it for love.

It was in the love I felt as I intuited and crafted, recollected and relived some of the best experiences of my own career in writing this book

---

[§] Gibran, Khalil. *The Prophet*. First published 1923; reprinted 143 times. New York: Alfred A. Knopf, 2007.

that I arrived at its title, returning to the famous Khalil Gibran quote which lived on my office door at Langara College for a number of years, and then which opened the home page on my first website in 1999 (alongside Ghandi's "Be the change you seek in the world"), and which today appears in calligraphy on the bulletin board which overhangs my desk: **"Work is love made visible."**

After two years of calling the manuscript "Values-Driven Careers," I realized that didn't cut it. It just didn't resonate enough. The point of values work is to focus very specifically on what you value. And love is my highest value; it's what I seek daily to bring to my work, and the title of this book needed to hold the love and joy I feel about it. Though my career is both *of* work and *about* work, I am not a workaholic and I don't aspire to be – not for myself and not for my career clients. Rather, I am a loveaholic, and great work is just one of the main ways I feed my addiction.

Love made visible: In those words live my dharma, my highest and most joyful calling, my values made succinct. I hope they speak to you, too.

Readers will find a hybrid of New Thought-influenced, affirmative thinking, life path, feel-the-fear-and-do-it-anyway personal growth content well mixed in with gap analysis, skill metrics, strategic planning, negotiating tactics, time maps and very practical advice. I believe in an authentic and integrated approach to work/life, with my highest self, head, heart, and hands working together harmoniously, thus even if the table of contents might have been simpler had the material been separated into neat boxes, the whole that is the book could be created no other way.

For many of you there will be parts of some chapters that are much easier to relate to or digest than others: early readers who gave me feedback tended to bemoan a perceived over-emphasis on "woo-woo" attraction and manifestation stuff while others felt the book was a little heavy on "how to" case studies and lost some of its heart in the details. And to both camps I say first thank you for reading, thank you for your careful consideration, thank you for mirroring for me the spectrum of viewpoints I myself hold... and I invite you to join with me in the spaces between and around the different points of view where we can meet, stretch out, fill up and make a new picture, intact and whole, together.

For me, the picture is still very much evolving. Indeed, my vision has been so fluid for several years now that I kept putting off publishing, thinking the day would come when my thinking would be fully formed. Then I began to realize that one of the greatest gifts I have ever known has been the lifelong learning I have always enjoyed and embraced, and I don't want that to change: with that clarity, that one fully formed thought making acceptance of many multiples of emerging thoughts possible, the book came together in just a few weeks. My next book will be another evolution; it may pick up where this one leaves off, yet it could just as easily take issue with it – or a little of both. I'm open either way.

I think that creating the work/life which will allow you to know, experience and contribute the best of yourself means embracing certain seeming contradictions and finding the perfection in their unique combination in you.

I invite you to be open to the idea that you can create any kind of life you want by first imagining it, then choosing to believe it is possible, then allowing it, and faithfully and joyfully working toward it as if it were already so.

I also invite your questions, comments and other feedback, sent to lovereaders@alannafero.com.

Where I speak of my own life and my own experiences in this book, it is important to note transparently that they are filtered through my own lens. I am well aware that others involved or witness to my experiences may have narrated them differently; indeed, at another time in my life or on another day in the future, I might as well. I have made every effort to tell my truth as I know it today and to be responsible and compassionate in so doing; I make no claims to telling "The Truth" for I know that no such thing exists.

Where I speak the experiences of my clients, I have made every effort to protect privacy and conceal identities. I live in Canada's third largest city, yet I find in my work it feels like a small town indeed, with most clients coming to me by personal referral and many turning up at similar conferences, events and other community activities. I care about them too much and feel too honoured by the very intimate sharing of their experience that they granted me to be anything less than extremely vigilant in how I share it with readers.

None of the names used in the book are the clients' actual names; in all cases I have also changed at least some details related to profession, industry, or family background; in many cases I have also changed gender and created some composite details out of a number of similar client experiences.

> I invite you to be open to the idea that you can create any kind of life you want by first imagining it, then choosing to believe it is possible, then allowing it, and faithfully and joyfully working toward it as if it were already so.

Reported conversations are based on notes, in most cases fairly detailed ones, but there is reconstruction from memory as well as transcription. I am confident that the experiences recounted and the lessons which may be extrapolated have no less relevance or veracity for the privacy measures and recollection employed, and I trust they will resonate for readers wanting to engage.

Readers will also note a liberal use of humour in the book: a few of my first readers of the manuscript worried for me that "others" might think I was laughing at people's struggles, making fun of confusion, resistance or pain. (These, of course, are the same people who wanted to know if they were maybe, you know, just a little bit, um, the basis for the case study in chapter X or Y?) Are you laughing yet?

Yes, there *is* a lot of laughter in the book: it's something I value highly. Laughter and joy are major drivers in my work, and my clients and I manage to have a very good time while we work through our struggles, resistance or pain. And I say "our" because there is no client experience in this book that I haven't had myself as well, and no progress or healing that wasn't made possible in part by finding the lightness in it. I report joking, cajoling, at times mocking someone's procrastination or teasing out ironies, simply because they happen. Where there is safety, trust, rapport, and intimacy, laughter is a natural by-product, and I take nothing more seriously.

You'll see that I also ask lots of pointed, provocative, even aggressive questions in the work: like the teasing and cajoling, the in-your-face "get real" approach only works when it has been earned over time and is balanced by gentleness and goodwill. Read these stories of laughter and tears with compassion, and then remember to extend that same compassion to yourself as you confront your own fears of change and growth. We're all making up our stories as we go along; the best we can do is offer loving narration and dare to be the heroes in our plot.

Readers will also note a marked absence of analyzing problems in this manuscript: I devote no space to describing for you what is not working about careers which are driven by models other than values – or, I suppose I should say driven by unconscious and perhaps unwanted values, since I firmly believe that values are everywhere and we are living by them whether we know it or not. The question is whether we allow ourselves to be swept up in the values of those around us or if we will choose to know and then to live by values which are authentically our own.

My academic training would tell me I have to spend several chapters describing case studies of people who have lost themselves in cultural drift and companies whose bottom line has been diminished by employee alienation and presenteeism in order to authoritatively establish the need for my thesis before acquiring permission to say what I have to say. While I am grateful for the development of an incisive mind made possible by my academic years, I think this model serves us not nearly as frequently as we use it – failing, as we often do, to simply imagine an alternative.

Our too frequent insistence on an academic, exhaustively researched model, teleological rather than exploratory, is not only a deterrent to good people feeling good about writing books and speaking on important topics, it is also wasteful and foolish in negating the collective wisdom we already have. Thankfully, many progressive academics are now bringing intuitive ways of knowing into their work, and to be fair I should say that it was in a university classroom where I was first introduced to these ideas and felt profound gratitude for the validation they brought.

And so we move forward. As David Korten, publisher of *YES!* Magazine and author of *The Great Turning*, recently said at a Business Alliance for Local Living Economies (BALLE) conference I attended: **"We are the ones we have been waiting for."**

We already know what isn't working – intuitively, viscerally, experientially, anecdotally and goodness knows academically and institutionally – we know already! Let's get on with it. It's time to rise above. This book seeks to not to avoid what's wrong or ignore the past but to accept it, integrate it and move on, focused on being present and looking forward: no problems, just solutions; no analysis, just ideas; no apologies, just affirmations; no seeking permission to speak, just claiming its voice as my – and *your* – birthright.

I hope you see yourself in this manuscript, and I invite you to take whatever inspiration you may find and use it to create the work/life you would most love to live.

Introduction:

Me and Maslow on Work/Life, Work/Love

Values. A word I must use in one context or another at least a hundred times a day. The V.I.P. Program: Values, Integrity and Purpose. Values-Based Time Management. Values-Driven Business. The Value of Energy and Engagement. Values-First Decision Making. A big part of my job is helping people to get in touch with – or even to access for the first time – what they value. As much as I work with this concept, I am routinely asked two questions: (1) What are values, really? and (2) How do I know what I really value?

I think the "really" aspect is as important as the "values" of these questions. In this digital information age so filled with virtual realities, our generation searches perhaps more than any before it for what is *real*. And values, in my view, if we open through them to our highest knowing of who we can imagine ourselves to be, are as real as it gets. Connecting with what you really care about, what matters, what excites, inspires and empowers you, what you can get behind, what you contribute, what you want to leave when your life is over, what you truly love . . . that's the *real* deal.

Values are absolutely foundational. Like the crawl space foundations on which our homes are built, however, for most of us values too often remain unconsidered in any conscious or intentional way until something appears dramatically out of balance (...or a bad smell alerts us to damage, decay and possible danger below...)

Values take the forms of knowing, beliefs, desires, philosophies, opinions, ethical principles, moral stances, political agendas, occupations, pastimes, personal styles, goals, material objects, emotions, people and relationships, and more... usually in combination. It's possible to desire or care about or work toward hundreds of these things throughout our lives, but *core values,* the highest and deepest ones that speak uniquely to our individual hearts, tend to come in sets of just five to ten. Fewer than five core values and we're probably not tapping into our whole, multi-faceted selves; more than ten and we've probably gone beyond what is essential into some sort of existential bonus round.

And once we know our values, we must then consider our values-in-action. Our lives are defined by the choices we make and the actions we take – and whether we allow and encourage our values to manifest at those levels. The good news is that it's possible to begin making more purposeful and principled choices at any time, as the people whose journeys you'll see described in this book have done. It's a simple yet profound truth that the greater the connection between our values and our activities, the higher the personal satisfaction we feel, the greater material and emotional abundance we enjoy, and the lower personal stress and stress-related illnesses we endure.

Taking stock of your values is thus central to taking care of yourself. More than that, it is a core component of self-actualization. As the great American psychologist Abraham Maslow tells us:

We can learn from self-actualizing people what the ideal attitude toward work might be under the most favourable circumstances. These highly evolved individuals assimilate their work into their identify of the self, i.e., work actually becomes part of the self, part of the individual's definition of self.

Maslow had no interest in exploration of the 'abnormal' or 'pathological' that we are usually made to study in first-year university survey courses. Maslow had the radical idea – astonishingly one of the first of its kind – to ignore neuroses and dysfunctions and diseases and instead to study happy, well-adjusted, successful people and see if there might be some lessons there for the rest of us.

Out of Maslow's early research was born his "hierarchy of human needs," in which basis safety and survival needs are at the bottom, a foundation which must be in place before we can go looking for much else, then growing upward through love, esteem, cognitive and aesthetic needs before culminating in the "self-actualization" to which all humans aspire and for which Maslow is best known. With self-actualization comes a series of "peak experiences": moments in which we know ourselves, feel in love with our lives, and deepen our humanity. The goal would be for those moments to become more lasting and more frequent until self-actualization is simply our limitless and unending state of being.

What even those who have studied Maslow often don't realize is that, over the course of his career, he came to believe that the context or venue in which self-actualization was most likely to be possible for the greatest number of people was *work*. Not family or intimate relationship because the people who love us often have a vested interest in who we will become. Not school because it more often serves to domesticate than free the soul. Not therapy because it's an experience that is not accessible to most people. Work, as common to all and constant in essence, even if shifting in particulars through most of a lifetime, would be where most people would 'find themselves.'§

§ See Abraham H. *Maslow, Maslow on Management* (New York: John Wiley & Sons, 1999) for excellent expansion on Maslow's research and hypotheses.

As Maslow wrote in his journals in the early 1960s, "All human beings prefer meaningful work to meaningless work. If work is meaningless, then life comes close to being meaningless." Meaningful work is thus seen as a path to living – and loving – fully, stepping into who we really are.

My own self-actualization comes in part from helping other people get closer to theirs. I started on this career path before I knew much more about Maslow than the diagram of his needs hierarchy memorized and reconstructed on some exam I must have written at 17 or 18 years of age. The discovery of the Maslow opus, decades of work on human potential and optimal experience, brought a peak moment to my own work/life, giving a context, deeper meaning and rich vocabulary to the self-actualizing story in which I was already a protagonist.

And so to my own vocabulary of this work, and what you can expect as the narrative of this book, I have come to think of my career philosophy – indeed, my very life philosophy – as a place where spirituality meets strategy, equal parts affirmative thinking and action plans. Idealistic pragmatism, really.

Bringing me great joy has been an emerging zeitgeist in our culture which recognizes values as serving us best at the centre of life, spirit at the forefront, and purpose as our barometer. Few people actually make reference to Maslow's language of self actualization, yet the majority of the people I meet and with whom I speak about my work quickly shift into dialogue about purpose, path, engagement, satisfaction, finding themselves, achieving life/work balance, feeling connected… The trend I most frequently and excitedly observe is a welcome recognition that we're all in this together, and workplaces are evolving to create intentional space for our work/life communities.

And even as I feel this commonality, and talk about a newly spirited spark at work, I spend a lot of time answering the question, "Um, what do you actually *do*?" Most of my clients come to me through other clients, and also from friends and associates and people who have seen me speak or read some of my work, and those people giving the referrals don't often explain what 'the work' is. They just say "You need to meet Alanna." They say it passionately and convincingly and their relationships with their friends and colleagues are such that people listen to them with great trust. So I get a mini parade of people calling or emailing me each week saying, "For some reason, so-and-so said I needed to contact you."

I smile, inside and out, and start asking the questions to find out where and how and to what degree I can be of service in their lives. Sometimes it turns out they don't need me – fortunately the people who know me or my work know that I never try to do something I can't do well (we're all here for a purpose and I'm clear on mine – working in an area that is not my passion only dilutes the impact I can have, so I know better.) They also know that I have a wonderful network of friends and associates to whom I can refer clients when they need another kind of expertise, so they'll get what they need one way or another. More often than not, though, one question builds on the one before it, and I find myself getting more and more excited as each answer reveals how we will begin to work together – me, my client, Maslow and the love we will share – to bring another self-actualized life all the way into its light and the world.

So much of what we do in life is shaped by the questions we are asked. When you were a kid, they asked you "What do you want to be when you grow up?" Unfortunately, the answers most of us gave – or were coached to give – were actually answers to "What do you want to do to make money?"

I ask my clients what they want to *be* – which includes expressing their innermost values, experiencing feelings, people, events and environments, and self-actualizing their deepest, most authentic selves – and then we work together to figure out what they'll do and where their money will come from, properly taking this experience of *being*, the felt sense of who they are that they want to manifest becoming true north on our psychic compass.

Because *my* being is at once imaginative and social, catalytic and optimistic, analytical and pragmatic, I am drawn to work which allows me to lend service in those ways. What I do is help people know who their heart and soul longs to be and then support them to do what they are.

People can create anything they want if they can just let themselves want it. Acceptance and letting go of inner conflict are the first prerequisites to making changes that bring dreams to life. You'll read stories of people who came to their career path by saying, "I know that life must have more to offer than what I'm doing now and I want you to help me find it," a powerful statement of faith and vision which makes the process go quite quickly if the 'visioneer' can stay in that confident consciousness throughout.

You'll also read about people who said, "Well, sure, I'd like to get paid $80,000 a year to work 25 hours per week on some amazing, creative project and then have all kinds of time left over to spend with my family and friends and long walks by the ocean, but that ain't gonna happen so

> **Our purpose is to support you to do the higher level, big picture, long term, centred and connected stuff ...that better reflects who you are and would seek to grow into.**

let's just focus on getting me a 55 hour a week job that doesn't suck as much as my current one and pays at least $50,000 a year so the bank doesn't foreclose our mortgage, okay?" As you might imagine, the journey from this starting place is often a little longer. But not necessarily so.

Sometimes the most transformative and transcendent experiences I have ever witnessed start with the most open hostility to the process: overt anger is actually easier to deal with than covert resistance because at least we can see what it is, engage with it, maybe even negotiate a little. The toughest cases are the ones where people are saying "Yes, I want to do this very much; let's get down to work!" with their minds and their mouths, all the while stuffing down a heart-based voice, whether it's trying to joyfully sing a different tune or softly say it's been hurt and is afraid. There are many variations on the vignettes sampled here, all of them ready to touch and inspire you if you will join the dance of allowing and acceptance along with the storytellers.

That I don't believe in quick fixes is not to say that I don't believe in – and regularly support the experience of – rapid growth, and you'll read those stories here, too. I know that when people allow themselves clarity on what they want, and open to the channels and tools before them to move into that desire – no matter how unfamiliar the experience appears to be at the outset – they can make dramatic and lasting changes at both inner and outer levels in a matter of just weeks or months. Consciousness can shift in an instant, and action in alignment with that consciousness can bring to life structure, resources and results which perfectly represent our vision in a small fraction of the time we might expect. *Surge, leap, bound, epiphany, awakening, transcendence:* these words exist because their possibility exists. Because someone imagined and then experienced them and chose to give language to their experience.

Discussions of the timelines of our work together notwithstanding, one of the first things I often tell my clients is not to confuse time with importance – the amount of time we spend on things is not reflective of their value: most of us, even those who have lots of energy and work very hard, spend more time sleeping than we do on any other single activity. Yet few of us would say sleep is more important to us than anything else; we simply know that we need to sleep a certain amount in order to do the other things that matter more to us, so we are willing to make that investment. Sleep is of limited value in and of itself; sleep is important because it serves a higher purpose. (You can see where I'm going here, right?)

Our days are full of activities and behaviours, some conscious but most simply habituated, which we allow to take up the lion's share of our lives, and which serve no purpose whatsoever – or, at least, no intentional purpose. A lot of people tell me that they would like to live in a more values-based or purposeful way, but there simply isn't time. That one always makes me chuckle. Our purpose in this work isn't to take all the stuff you're already juggling and then add another 300% more to it and watch you get hit in the head by stray balls. This is neither game nor torture. Our purpose is to support you to do the higher level, big picture, long term, centred and connected stuff that will review and evaluate everything you are doing, and then keep and support what is on-purpose and replace what is not with plans and activities — a *life* not just a living — that better reflects who you are and would seek to grow into.

Figure one shows what I mean: the top is the most important and should direct the rest, but each item's relative size also reflects the proportion of time it needs in order to guide and serve you. The bottom, so much bigger, is where you will invest most of your time and energy, but its position in the hierarchy reveals that it is result not cause. (You know the small print in any contract is always the most important, right?)

Values & Purpose, and the spirit centre from which they spring, are properly at the top, followed by the heart-centred areas of Passions, Visions and Intention and Daydreaming, Creative Expression and opportunities for your intuition and subconscious to come out and play. That doesn't mean that I see your life playing out in an ashram or on a therapist's couch. Rather, it means that you need to invest enough time and energy for a couple of days once a year, and then a few minutes each day, to get and stay in touch with these life drivers and allow them to guide you and propel you forward.

If your life at times feels like it is spinning in circles or like you are racing very fast in one direction only to find yourself right back where you started (and were trying to escape), my contention is that it is likely because you are missing out on the directional gifts that these higher ways of knowing and guiding yourself offer you.

In the middle zone of the graphic is where we put our thinking caps on: Prioritizing, Framing and Leveraging (thus making decisions about how we will choose to see, engage with and act on the values & intention we identify) and Strategy, Planning & Scheduling (once we know what we care about and what among those passions is most important to us, how will we choose to allocate time, energy, resources and attention to it? And how will we get the support we need to make it easier? To integrate the pieces into a whole life rather than a fragmented one?). And because this is an area which shifts and changes more than the spiritual and emotional levels which inform it, it naturally needs more time and space.

Here I find myself attracted to the metaphors offered by sailing: we set a course, a more or less straight shot to our destination, and then the winds and the waves have their way with us so that the journey, the actual experience of sailing, is one of constant course correction. To that

Figure One

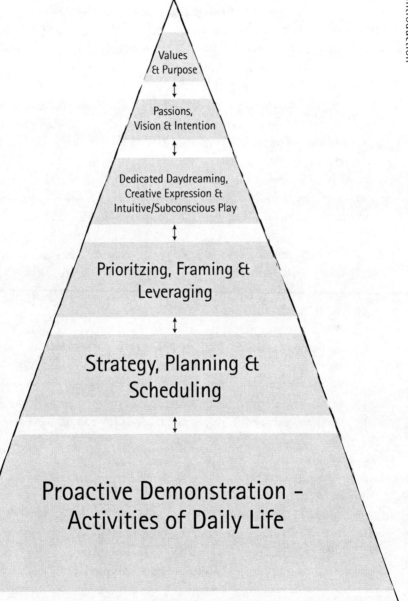

Values
& Purpose

Passions,
Vision & Intention

Dedicated Daydreaming,
Creative Expression &
Intuitive/Subconscious Play

Prioritzing, Framing &
Leveraging

Strategy, Planning &
Scheduling

Proactive Demonstration -
Activities of Daily Life

I would add a regular checking in to make sure that we do not sail past a better island than that for which we set sail, but rather remain open to our landscape and the very real possibility that we may get where we want to be in a different way or well ahead of schedule. And any skilled yachtsman would also suggest having a good look at our hull now and then to make sure we are not carrying anything unwanted with us to drag down our easy flow in the water.

Finally, grounding it all is the realm of the physical and material: the Proactive Demonstration of who we are and what we care about that takes the form of our creations, activities of daily life, that which we build from our intentions – if, that is, we are remembering to pay attention to intention! And this is the big, bold print, both in the literal sense of the text on this page and the figurative sense of what shows up in the world and is most easily visible as expression of what we love – and of our selves *as love.*

For our demonstrations of self to be good, to be authentic, to fill and feed us and the world to which we offer our gifts, we must qualitatively give enough energy and time to the top of the triangle so we may quantitatively give enough energy and time to the right things at its base.

And those bi-directional arrows? They're there because, even as I believe that our primary orientation is top down, I also know that our experience of our vision in life, values in action, love made visible, begins to inform our intention as well. Eventually, the two dialogue together, become friends, and enrich the meaning and joy of one another. I could well have added arrows moving in other directions, too, as we encounter and share the purposes, passions, plans and play of the other lives we allow to touch our own, shaping our selves and our worlds through our connections and communities. The graphic is simplified: your life will be rich with many layers.

If this seems obvious to you because you are already living in this way, great! Thanks for coming to the party. You'll love seeing your journey transcribed here, like photos from a beloved vacation. If instead it is feeling somewhat foreign, that's great, too. Because this party is for you – a barn-raising in the style of my prairie grandparents – and you'll soon have a lot of new friends on these pages, people who have built what you are seeking to build and who can share their design and construction tips and help you feel supported to create the very best that you can.

The key to allowing and creating work/life (or any) change is to be more attracted to your values, purpose, vision and intention than you are attached to your habits, patterns, doubts and other underserving aspects of your life. You need to imagine a future so clearly and in such rich detail that your feelings in the present are those you experience in the future — that's how you bring your future to life in the moment. See it, smell it, feel it, touch it, here and now, and then begin acting from that state.

And acting from that state in my own life is exactly how this book came to be. To make the book in my heart's desire and mind's eye the real thing you are reading, I had to find all the love to make it visible. The book came to full fruition and my practice began to fill, then develop a waiting list from time to time, when I realized that my purpose was not "helping people get things done" as many people had been interpreting it and I had not clarified or corrected, but rather "helping people feel like they can do anything and then take action in organic expression of that knowing about themselves." A much higher and more inspiring mission — for me and for my clients.

I still give people tools and tactics and guidance. But I understand that my gift comes from and touches people at spirit and heart levels first and last. Mind and body, thought and action, are important support through the middle of the work and may even take up the lion's share of the time and output in the end, but should not be confused as focal points in process or importance. The day that clicked in was empowering, uplifting, loving, expansive... and so easy it made me laugh out loud that I hadn't seen it sooner!

And so to introduce this work there are no better words than these poetic lines of love:

> When you work you are a flute through
> whose heart the whispering of the hours
> turns to music...
>
> Always you have been told that work is a
> curse and labour a misfortune.
> But I say to you that when you work
> you fulfill a part of earth's furthest dream,

assigned to you when that dream was born,
    And in keeping yourself with labour you
are in truth loving life,
    And to love life through labour is to be
intimate with life's inmost secret...

    All work is empty save when there is love;
    And when you work with love you bind
yourself to yourself, and to one another,
and to God...

    Work is love made visible.

                    - Kahlil Gibran, *The Prophet*

Chapter 1

Jump and the Net Will Appear:

Moving Your Career Forward Before You Know Where You Are Going

I came across the work of British psychologist Richard Wiseman[§] a few years ago and have at some point made pretty much every single client I have worked with since listen to my two minute snapshot of his longitudinal research study on Luck. My personal belief is that what Wiseman speaks of (is everybody catching his name, by the way?!) is really faith and the creative power that comes from a spiritual connection, but talking about it in terms of luck is more culturally inclusive, more widely accessible to a

---

[§] Richard Wiseman, *The Luck Factor: Changing Your Luck, Changing Your Life.* Century, 2003.

diverse client mix, and I find I can say it in a way that all of them relate to it. It's what my friend Kerry calls my spiritual utilitarianism kicking in: I don't care where an idea comes from or what we choose to name it; as long as I experience it as positive and helpful, and it can serve my clients' best lives and highest selves, I can get on board!

So the smart and prescient Mr. Wiseman followed two demographically diverse control groups of people over a long stretch of time (at least a year, if memory serves). One group was made up of people who self-identified as very or extremely *lucky* on a scale measuring relative perception of luck in life, and the other group – you guessed it – self identified as very or extremely *unlucky*. Wiseman and his team took detailed life histories, observed their subjects' choices and interactions, looked for patterns in their narration and journaling of their day-to-day experiences and, in my favourite part of the study, also brought the subjects into the research lab for some controlled experiments. Each individual was given a special copy of a newspaper and asked to count the number of photographs in the front section. Though many were puzzled at the purpose and relevance of such an activity, all did as they were asked.

100% of the test subjects who had self-identified as *unlucky* correctly counted the number of photographs as 43 in round about two to three minutes and left the research facility, many no doubt still shaking their heads, not understanding any more than perhaps you do now why this is significant. Here it comes: over 90% of the respondents who believed they were *lucky* finished in just a couple of seconds. And they did not count all the way to 43. Overwhelmingly, they stopped on page two and handed in their paper without counting further. The caption on that page? In something like 72 point font – extra large front page headline size, letters over two inches high – it read "You can stop counting now. There are 43 photographs in the newspaper." And if anyone missed that, there was another jumbo caption about half-way through, reading "There are 43 photographs. Hand the paper in to the attendant now and collect $250."

The unlucky group had the same opportunity to find an easy answer or enjoy a windfall; they simply couldn't see it. The lucky ones were people who expected the world to offer up gifts to them, which gave them a heightened awareness and allowed them to see and receive the opportunity and reward.

And can't you just hear the voices of the unlucky group when they were shown the newspaper headline they missed? Had to be a trick: the print really couldn't have been that big and obvious when they were given the paper. And how come no one told them to look for hidden messages? They were only asked to count photographs, after all. Yes, and knowing that all the lucky people sailed through to glory and cash prizes, you may be tempted to judge Wiseman's unlucky control group harshly, and think that could never be you.

About you, I can't say. I *can* say that the majority of my clients, even those who have the most positive and productive attitudes and beliefs with respect to their careers and their lives, either start out thinking that their purpose is a deep secret to be bestowed on them in a great white light upon death, or not-so-secretly maintaining that the job market is rigged in some way, or eventually succumb to a brief period of thinking that it's not fair that some jobs are filled behind closed doors, that there are "tricks" to the interview process, that some people are just luckier or more focused or more gifted than they are and there is nothing to be done about it... There is a level on which they want me to take them into some clandestine ceremony and reveal the career wisdom of the ages in a cloud of frothy smoke. Or – even worse, in my view – some want me to just do it for them, Poof, new life! Personal enlightenment not required. I assure you that by the end of any first hour with me, these perceptions have been well and thoroughly disabused, and I continue to challenge any recurrence of such beliefs, equally untrue and unhelpful, whenever they pop back up. I also completely accept that they will pop up in every life, including mine. Which is why we must choose again, recommit, in each moment.

The 72 point font is there for all of us, if we believe it can be. Worry less about squinting to see the small print in life and instead choose to simply to open your eyes to a world full of giant headlines bearing good news for those who have adjusted to the light.

Because there is no small controversy around this question of opportunistic small print in certain corners of my profession, bear with me while I digress into a brief but, I feel, necessary rant to emphatically say: *There is NO hidden job market.* Many laypersons, career professionals of one stripe or another, and a disproportionate sampling of media and government sources are in love with that phrase – to the detriment of any reader or viewer who crosses their path. I don't know who started it but I would really like to give them a good swift... ahem... *suggestion* that there are more helpful metaphors for people who are already going through one of life's major challenges than to give them the impression that some hostile and malevolent entity out there is deliberately obscuring and withholding opportunity from them at a critically vulnerable time in their lives.

To be clear (like I've been subtle so far, right?), my objection is not just that the notion of a "hidden job market" is unkind (which it is) but more than that - it's just plain dumb! It's like saying that China is hidden because you can't see it from North America or Europe. Unadvertised jobs are not hidden – they just don't come looking for you when your eyes are closed. And neither you nor your ideal career path are 'lost' and waiting for you to 'find' yourself. No opportunity would ever wait. They do not just sit around, static, hoping to be noticed. Opportunities are fluid, dynamic, and attracted by people who are also fluid and dynamic, ready to create and manifest, believing that they can.

Wanna get lucky? Start by knowing that luck is a choice you can make every day.

I think luck shows up in my work most as *ease* – a fluid kind of knowing that all is well as a client moves forward. It's not an absence of work: in fact there is great challenge. It's an absence of struggle. Anyone and everyone can succeed if they continue to learn, grow and act, even as they experience difficulty. The clients who succeed with the greatest *ease*, though, manage to encounter difficulty without having a difficult experience. Can you see the subtle difference? They ascribe a different meaning to events, and they are resilient to any setback. Simply: they choose luck and their luck takes the form of ease and that ease leads to success more expediently and joyfully than what can be experienced without it.

One might assume that people who had made a major career transition before might be better at it – succeed more easily, that is. Or those who have a strong background in coaching, counselling or another field related to human performance? Or perhaps even marketing, advertising or self promotion? Nope, within that group there are those who sail through and just as many who kick and scream all the way. Other readers might guess that transitions are easier when they are made by choice rather than circumstance, or where the client has a strong background or network in

> **Worry less about squinting to see the small print in life and instead choose to simply to open your eyes to a world full of giant headlines bearing good news for those who have adjusted to the light.**

the field to which they seek entry, or perhaps if they have a very supportive spouse and strong social ties. Big nuh-uh again. I could give you an equal number of examples of clients who fit that profile and had a very bumpy ride as those who would describe their experience as a relative cake walk.

When I look for something which separates clients in terms of either or both the quantity of time for their transition (say, benchmarking at ten weeks or less versus sixteen weeks or greater to really differentiate them) and their perceived quality of their experience (some version of "time of my life" versus some version of "is it over yet?"), the distinguishing factor is their belief in the process as I laid it out, and, more significantly, their belief in themselves and the world. Clients who succeed with luck and ease, who transition gracefully, believe in their own talents, abilities and attractiveness in the world. They also believe, often though not always with equal conviction, that the world is on their side, that things generally go their way, and that they can feel safe in expecting a good experience.

Do the members of this illustrious group maintain this Zen-like faith and awareness from day one to a blissful union with their new work/life, after which they never doubt themselves again? No. There is no need. I'll help them with ideas, strategy, planning, implementation, negotiation, all that practical stuff. More importantly, I serve to hold the faith, hold the space of believing — hold their place in the "It's all good" line while they deke out for an "I know I know better but today it's really hard and I'm too scared to make sense or be consistent" break. Holding that space is never more important than for the client who dares to let go of what s/he has before having any clear idea of what comes next.

Such willingness to step off a known career path as a way to be open to something better is of course more often the province of people who see themselves as lucky than those who don't, yet everyone will be tested by the experience. I think of these clients as my Joseph Campbell team: Heroes with a Thousand Faces, courageously trekking into the wilderness to find out what they are made of. "Jump and the Net Will Appear," "Leap and Sprout Angel's Wings": these are the expressions of those who have landed and landed well. They are rarely the words on our lips as we stare over the precipice into the unknown. But for Alistair, one special client with whom I greatly enjoyed working, it was those words and more like them: bold, faith-full, and completely ready to deal with not being ready. A great place from which to begin, and to revisit along the journey.

Alistair came to me a few weeks after he had, in the space of just a few days, given two months' notice at his job and signed up for a three month yoga retreat near Puna, India. "I don't know what's next but I know I will die inside if I don't decide to start living *now*," Alistair proclaimed in his first email to me. He had spent his entire adolescent and adult life in the pursuit of one expansive goal: to fully understand and add to the *collective* understanding of post-colonial history, this leading to an endowed chair in History at a major university. "Twenty-two years," he said, when we met.

"Twenty-two years of books and films and interviews and papers about the birth of new societies in former colonies. Nine years of university alone! Growing up British, learning all about Empire, I was fascinated by the impulse to control another culture and the stronger impulse of that culture to be free. Even at 14 and 15 years old, I had to understand it," Alistair said. And understand it he did. Alistair had authored one book (his PhD dissertation immediately accepted for publication in its entirety as a book, a coup in itself), as well as a number of scholarly articles in peer-reviewed journals, and he was working on a second book-length manuscript. He was an assistant professor at a prestigious Canadian university (the closest our young, post-colonial country gets to an Ivy League!), and up for the tenure that would put one last check mark on the lofty list of career goals he had developed so early in life. The brass ring of an academic career was within his grasp.

There was just one thing: he didn't want it anymore.

"I can't stand the bullshit politics," he railed. "Committees and scholarships and fellowships and grants... always jockeying for position, always having to kiss ass quoting the right people before I can say what I think. And the prize is I get to stay and keep doing it for the rest of my life? That sounds like jail, not promotion." Even in professions that don't have so rigid an employee engagement system as academic tenure, there is nothing like getting exactly the security we think we want to make us rethink that wanting. I see clients have this experience all the time: Money? Check. Status? Check. Challenge? Check. Home? Check. Family, car, vacation, hobbies? Check, check, check. Happiness? Uh oh. Where did I go wrong?

That's not really the question, of course. It's more like "Where did I go?" As Alistair noted, "I was so busy going after what I wanted, I didn't notice I wasn't the same me anymore. So naturally I wouldn't want the same things. Yet it's like I couldn't see that until I had them all." I told him that was very common. In all the busy-ness and striving, there is precious little reflection. He saw who he was when all the achieving slowed down enough to allow him to be still and take a look. "You don't think it's a coincidence you took up yoga at the same time your name was put forward to the tenure committee, do you?" I asked.

"I guess not," Alistair smiled. But then his smile faded: "So much time wasted. I don't know how I'm going to make a living as a yoga teacher – I'll probably have to sell the house – but at least I'll be me. If we can get a job lined up for me before I go, maybe with a studio that doesn't currently offer the kind of yoga I'll be certified in, then I can relax and focus on learning."

By this time we had done a fair amount of values-clarification, skills audits, personality assessments, and talked – at a very deep level – for about six sessions. I felt like I knew Alistair well enough to throw my two cents all the way in. "You know, about that... my gut tells me you maybe won't actually make a *career* out of being a yogi," I said, wading in gently.

"You think I'm on the wrong path?" Alistair rushed to question.

"On the contrary," I said, "I think you're on exactly the right path. I just *also* think you'll probably keep moving. If you recall when we first met, you weren't actually saying you thought that yoga was your true calling. It was kind of an 'anywhere but here' response when you gave notice, and you picked something structured, enjoyable, reflective and in a country you love: all impulses toward safety and social connection which can give you a foundation for the self-actualization you seek. Good instincts. I just think they're the beginning and not necessarily the end."

"But this isn't just a vacation. I'm getting certified. I'll have credentials," came Alistair's weak attempt at a rebuttal.

"Are you really going to sit there with a PhD and a couple of post-docs racked up and tell me you're worried about a three month yoga certificate?" I asked, and he grinned immediately. "I'm thinking you might be past needing any more letters after your name. Someday, for practical reasons, maybe. But you don't need that kind of validation here: your brain has already been declared officially 'full.' My guess is you picked a school instead of just a spa because you relate to learning, to study. It's a way of being in the world that is familiar to you. And when we're doing something that is totally new to us, we're already so far outside of our comfort zone. We can use a little familiarity in some of our methods, tools or people so we can balance all that newness. I say again: your instincts were great. You made a great decision. And I'm excited for you taking the trip and the course. I'm simply inviting you to be open to whatever experience you have and not attached to knowing you are going to become a yoga teacher. In studying yoga, you will study yourself. Go get a PhD in you. Come back and tell me what you learn. If you learn your calling is to own a yoga studio, I'll not only help you set it up and market it, I'll buy your first membership. And if you learn something else, I'm here for that, too."

And so off Alistair went, renting out rather than selling his home, and, after convincing his girlfriend to join him, extending his three month stay to almost five months before returning.

"I know what I want to do!" he announced proudly when I saw him again. "I want to be a game producer."

"Like educational games? Board games? Stuff for kids?" I queried from my frame of reference.

> A consciousness of lack is a problem and needs to be addressed, shifted to one of possibility and abundance. But *actual* lack is just an opportunity, an open space to be filled as you would intend.

"Nope," he giggled (that alone a first). "Like 'Where in the World Is Carmen San Diego?,' 'Civilization,' and 'Discovering Babylon.' Interactive video games. Simulations. Virtual Reality. Digital worlds."

"Wow!" I said.

"Really!" he said. And we both knew he meant it.

Object lesson for all readers: never be dissuaded from a career path by lack of experience, lack of credentials, lack of contacts. A consciousness of lack is a problem and needs to be addressed, shifted to one of possibility and abundance. But *actual* lack is just an opportunity, an open space to be filled as you would intend. Alistair, as you might have guessed given his background, had never produced anything before. He had certainly never designed or project managed development of a video game. In fact, he had even only played a few video games!

But he felt inspired, called. He was certain that all of his experience in the study of how new worlds are created, how populations of people become self-governing, self-sustaining and self-respecting, could inform the conception of virtual worlds which would excite, inspire and even sell. (That last part was a revelation to him. "I never really thought about money before! Academics are paid on a step scale – you don't negotiate, at least not until you are up for Chair or Dean. But I've been reading all these books about business and I think my games even have a revenue model! The business part isn't even that scary – my Dad was a corporate lawyer so I grew up around people doing deals. My becoming an academic broke his heart, poor guy. He's going to hate this, too, but I'll get him on board! I know this can work!" he said gleefully.)

My work compels me to follow the glee.

And so began a strategic plan in which Alistair got to know all of the gaming companies in our region, as well as the largest global competitors. He bought and played dozens of video games, much to his girlfriend's not-well-hidden dismay ("Professor turned 'Gamer' is a pretty big jump," she would ironically observe. "Reading is such a quiet activity by comparison." Yes, *and* dreams demand support, even if all one can do is smile and nod while wearing earplugs.) Alistair read up on film and video, too, and leveraged introductions to a couple of other clients of mine to get himself on some film sets and sit in on some production meetings to see how these kinds of creative projects come together. He read endless pages of industry magazines, surfed chatrooms, subscribed to blogs, and devoured books on arts- and technology-based businesses. He was a kid in a candy store. And, like most kids who indulge in a sugar binge, he eventually got a tummy ache.

"What are we doing?" he asked, slumped in his chair, staring blankly at the table. "I mean, really, is there any point to this? It's fun – or it was for awhile – but how is game immersion going to turn into a job? Who is going to hire me because I've read the latest posts in some cybergeek periodical?"

"No one," I said, as Alistair looked aghast.

"Come now, I'm not telling you anything you don't already know," I said. "Nothing we haven't talked about many times. No one hires anyone because of what they have read or even because of what they have studied or what they have done before. Not good hiring, anyway. Not the kind of place you're going to want to work. People hire people they like, who share their values and passions, and who they can imagine growing their skills and abilities in service of the vision they have for where their organization is going. As we always said, you have to talk to those people to make this happen. It will be about relationships – it always is. And you couldn't talk to them until you learned their language. Since half the time I can't understand what you're saying anymore, I think you've learned it well enough to start some exploratory conversations!"

Laughing with me, Alistair pulled out his laptop full of research and opened the database file with the gaming contacts we'd been compiling. Together we drafted tightly structured letters of introduction to five of the lower level people on his list: structure to keep his message authentic and on-point, not overwhelming to the reader (easy to do when he has so much pent up enthusiasm looking for an outlet) and crafted a phone script to get him through those first few calls asking for a meeting. It all sounds very contrived, I know, but we need structure when we are heading into unknown territory. As it gets more familiar, we can take more latitude.

My goal for every client is for them to find not just their own path but also their own authentic voice – indeed, their own way of being, of doing everything. Since they have to start moving before they get there, though, my version of their voice acts like training wheels: my plans and scripts balance for them until they gain momentum and confidence to do it for themselves.

After his first week of relationship-building, Alistair was again filled with glee, breathless as he caught me up on all his happenings: "These people are so NICE! The first person I talked to said he had received my letter and was intrigued – intrigued! – by my background. We talked for a few minutes on the phone and he is letting me take him to coffee next week. I only got the receptionist at two of the companies, but it felt good just to be trying, you know? And I had a meeting just before I came here with a junior production coordinator at one of the big five companies we talked about. She actually started out as a fitness instructor, then did some event planning, met someone from the company and was brought on board when they decided to do some virtual trainer programs for the fitness industry. She didn't know gaming, either, but they gave her a shot. This is possible! It's *actually possible*!!!"

I know! I love these days! Opening to the possible is even richer for me than opening to the actual – the *decision* to succeed more important than the success itself. Any job is just a one-time thing, potentially career-only. Belief, powerful, in-your-bones knowing that you can make things happen for yourself? That's transforming, and it's yours to take into every area of your life. That's why I do this work.

And as much as we were enjoying it, I've also been doing this long enough to know that the level of change Alistair was sampling right now doesn't sink in over just a day or a week, and that career transition doesn't happen in two or three warm and fuzzy networking meetings, either. Without being a buzzkill, I had a responsibility to let Alistair know a little about the road ahead of him so he could be prepared.

I started slow: "These are exciting times, huh? Those first few tastes of connection in your new community are so sweet. I'm very happy for you. And for homework, I want you to record, in as much detail as you can remember, everything that happened this week and exactly how you feel. Write down the parts about how nice people are, how effortless it is, how much possibility you feel in that young woman's story of her success, how much your confidence is growing, how you know where you are going – you can see it, feel it, trust it. And then I want you to write some advice to yourself, based on how you are feeling today, but directed to yourself on a day which didn't go as well, when you might be forgetting how good this can feel. Write a letter telling yourself what you will need to hear to get back to this hopefulness, this knowing in yourself, the faith to get up and move on, even on a day when the road is a little bumpier."

Alistair bravely hung on to his smile – a lot of clients wouldn't at this point – and said "But you'll remind me, right?"

"Of course I will," I replied. "But some days you might not believe me." He looked like he didn't believe me now. "I've seen a few clients sail through so beautifully that no one is ever impatient or short with them and an offer comes in a matter of days. I truly hope you're one of them – nothing would make me happier. But I've seen enough to know that those are the outliers. It's my job to tell you what is typical. And typical looks like weeks or even months of making friends and associates out of very busy and distracted strangers. No matter how well you do it, there will be days when no one says yes to coffee or when a meeting is perfunctory because they are thinking about ten other things. And on those days, some clients would choose to feel like it's all crashing; nothing works; their early successes were dumb luck and now they're over and they should just give up. And it used to take me days, sometimes even weeks, to support them recalibrating to a positive place from which we can do the work. I've learned I can help the vast majority of clients skip that crash by preparing them for the possibility of a small dip in their energy, and having them create the tools they will need to rebalance and keep themselves elevated before it even comes up. And if we never need them, you'll still have written a beautiful journal to look back on when this is all over – you can read it to your grandkids."

"I guess that makes sense," Alistair mumbled weakly, not liking this but game to stay with me at least.

"It comes down to understanding that you can choose to feel this good every day," I said. "You might never need that letter to yourself. But if you slip – and many people do, just for a little while, nothing wrong with that, just part of being human, getting let down sometimes when we are vulnerable because we care – you'll be ready to deal. I'm here, of course, but my job is to support you to be self sufficient. The best messages are from you to you."

Alistair wrote the letter. Seventeen typewritten pages, I believe. It didn't actually have footnotes, but, bless him, it read like it should have. Hey, use whatever strengths you've got, I say. His skills included the ability to connect every dot in chronological order and ascribe causality to key events in history: he had a whole analysis of his great week ready for replication. And mostly he did replicate it, keeping his energy pretty high through well over a dozen more networking meetings, diligent follow-up, more research, starting to get clearer about what he wanted. Until the day his Dad said, "It's been four months since you got back from India, son. You're using up all your savings on this pipedream. When are you going to wake up and go back to your real life?"

Few of us can face that kind of judgment from an authority in our lives, someone we want to be proud of us, and not feel somewhat shaken. And Alistair had just been taking a look at his bank balance, and also taking some heat from friends who wanted to be supportive, but who really couldn't understand what he was doing. Even the most well-meaning people in our lives are not *in* our experience. They can't see it from our perspective. Some of them maybe have their own agenda for who they are prepared to let us become, wanting our lives to meet their needs and expectations. Most are more benign in intent, though, and just think they are protecting us by encouraging us to be realistic to avoid getting hurt. And even knowing all that, what they say still hurts in the moment, doubly so at such a vulnerable time. Alistair's head was spinning.

"Maybe they're right," he said. "I've been screwing around with this. Sure, people have been nice. Sure, I'm getting lots of meetings. I'm learning, whatever. But I'm thinking that I really need to go to design school or some computer geek training or something if I want to do this. Or I should just go back to the university. Who is really going to let a historian make games? Who were we kidding?"

"I don't think we were kidding anyone, Alistair," I replied. "And you don't think so, either. What you *do* think is that it really hurts to be spoken to the way your Dad spoke to you. And it's really scary to be so out in the open right now, not sure where shore is going to be." I paused so he could take that in. "It's appropriate to be scared right now. You've known your whole life – since you were 14 years old, for goodness sake! – what you were going to do. And now you don't know, at least not for sure. Anyone would be shaken up by that. But let's talk about what's shaking you, not conclude that this means you are on some fool's errand, kidding yourself, waiting to wake up. Because we both know that's not what's happening here."

"I have a house, a mortgage. I'm not a kid anymore," he said.

"Grown men get scared, too. In fact, they're the prototype. You studied all those great leader biographies: Prime Ministers and Generals, lives in the balance. It ain't courage if you're not scared," I replied.

"Can you tell me for sure this is going to work?" Alistair asked.

"You know I can't," I answered.

"Then how do I know I'm doing the right thing?" he said, as softly as I had ever heard him speak.

"The same way you knew you loved History when you were young," I said. "And the same way you knew it was time to leave academe. The same way you knew Helen was the one for you. The same way you decided to work with me. The same way you chose the yoga school. And the same way you knew your path is to take all that historical knowledge you've crammed into your brain and put it onscreen for kids to play and learn at the same time. Look through your heart, not your fear. You know."

We got through that day, Alistair and I, and a few more like it over another six weeks of high highs and medium lows. He never flat-out crashed, always called or emailed when he felt his energy slipping, getting a boost in time instead of giving in to the fall. And one day his email was very excited.

"I did what you said. I sent a thank you letter saying I would like to explore how we could add a new line of virtual society games to their product line – some Second Life type code and a few other ideas – super casual – just 'perhaps we could find a convenient time to explore mutual interests,' I know how you love that phrase, and THEY WENT FOR IT!!! They asked me to come back with my resume and a brief proposal for a meeting with three of their senior people! Now what do I do?"

Another good day! Just like possibility, anticipation and excitement are also better for me than the closure of a negotiation or deal. What can be, what will grow. These are my passions. We worked out highly company-specific tweaks to the resume and language for a proposal, along with a powerpoint presentation, and off he went. He called me giddy when he was done: "I was good! It was great! They said they'd call me in a couple of days. I've got the thank you ready to send."

I congratulated him and told him to keep me posted. A week later and they hadn't called. Alistair was crestfallen, saying "I guess I'm not what they're looking for after all."

Not so fast. "Did you deliver the presentation as we outlined it?" I asked.

"Yes."

"We know the presentation was good. Did they ask lots of specific questions?" I explored further.

"Yes."

"Those are solid signs of engagement. Were they sitting up, taking notes, cross talking with each other about your ideas, about possible implementations?"

"Yes."

"Those are solid signs of buy-in. Did they mention anything about what has been going on in their business?"

"Yes. In a previous meeting they were talking about closing a new distribution deal," Alistair recalled.

"Ah," I said. "Now we're getting somewhere. Change your filter for a minute: stop thinking about all the ways your dream is collapsing and start thinking about all the perfectly ordinary reasons that the most senior people in a rapidly growing but small company could be too busy to call you for a couple of days. What have you got?"

"They were all working on major projects. And one had a bad cold. And we did meet on a Friday which means they probably got slammed with work on Monday and the week got away from them," Alistair said. "But we don't know that's the reason..." he added.

"No, you're right about that," I replied. "But we can't know what the reason is. You can't call them up to ask so you've got to get through this on your own. Your 'I must not have been as good as I thought' reason will make you feel bad, ruin your week, and come through in any communication you might have with them going forward. My 'they are busy; they mean well; they simply over-promised' reason will make you feel okay, let you move on, and make you sound mature and casual when you talk to them. When you can't know what the facts are, I say forget fact and focus on optimistically pragmatic perception. Tell yourself the story that will be the most helpful and move on. With that in mind, I want you to get back to talking to at least three other companies this week."

"But you said not to give up on this," argued Alistair. "I want to be ready when they call."

"You'll be ready. But you won't be sitting around. The best way not to sound desperate when you talk to them is to actually *not be* desperate. Create some other opportunities, liven up, boost your energy, and when you tell them 'Gee, I have a few things going on but I think I can probably come by towards the end of the week,' it will actually be true. Visualize what you want and make it true. You want to be a guy with a number of attractive options to choose from, so let's make that happen, okay?"

And back to work he went. They did call, a full two weeks later, what would have been absolute agony in waiting if Alistair hadn't been exploring other options, and they apologized profusely. One had missed three days of work due to illness; another called away on a client emergency; the third left holding the bag. Nothing to do with Alistair at all. And he could truthfully say, "Yes, I thought it had to be something like that. Don't worry about it. I had lots on my plate as well." He was their peer, not some underling waiting around to be told what to do. "Jumping" means trusting the net will appear. We don't wait for the fire department to show up with a ladder or parachute. It's bold. Boldness is what got Alistair this far, and boldness is what it would take to finish it.

Although they were apologetic and still expressed some interest in him, the R&D director was so swamped with work, he wanted to put off follow-up discussions until after close of the quarter, and was saying things like "We completely understand if you need to pursue other options. We wouldn't presume to tie you up for so long." Again, that hit hard.

"Maybe they are just being polite, giving me a kiss-off," Alistair wondered as he recounted his phone call.

"Sure," I said. "It could be a corporate case of 'It's not you; it's me. You deserve more than I can offer. You should see other people,' for sure."

"But you always say to assume the best intentions! They could be telling the truth!" Alistair sputtered.

"Yup," I said, "and since you know that full well, it was about time you got there on your own!" We both smiled.

Our plan went like this: believe them and solve their problem. After we worked out the strategy together, Alistair drafted a proposal and a memo of understanding which outlined a six month initial contract term during which he would work with a mid-level member of their R&D team on a specific concept discussed in their meeting. He specified that either party could back out on four weeks' notice if it wasn't working, and that a successful meeting of mutually defined objectives at the end of the six months would result in moving to negotiation of a full year contract, then a permanent full time one. He said he understood that they had a lot on their plates and he wanted to make things easier to move forward if indeed there was interest. It's the kind of initiative they could expect him to take as part of their organization if they brought him on board. All casual, no numbers, just an email with an attachment and a promise of a follow-up call within 24 hours.

They liked his initiative. Terms were easy to negotiate. Where we might have expected Alistair to take as much as a 60% pay cut in an entry level position just to get into the industry – in fact, we had even discussed a 90 day unpaid internship if that's what it would take to break in – by being open to working on contract *and* initiating the proposal himself, Alistair took only a 20% hit and was able to negotiate a mid-level sounding title and promise of multiple evaluations and references. However it worked out, he would be ahead of the game with lots of achievements from his new industry to begin his new resume.

As luck would have it, the relationship is developing well. Alistair is completing phase one of the contract and loving what he is doing so far. He's also a big convert to the world of holding faith and acting as if you believe it will all work out. No evangelist like the newly converted! Let the glee continue...

Chapter 2

~~Frustrated~~ *Fabulous!* ∨ Artists:

Creative Career Paths

We all know the story of the 'frustrated artist,' right? The wildly creative person who somehow gets stuck in the wrong life, pushing a broom or shuffling paper, just trying to make ends meet, dying a little every day as they sacrifice to pay the bills... cue violins and filmic montage of wistful seamstress looking plaintively at the flowers out the window and wishing her life could be different...

Enough, already! Once upon a time it may have been necessary for some people in some cultures to sell their souls short for a meal but, if you are reading this book, chances are you are not one of them. And as a culture, it's time we stopped making a virtue of soul-strangulating sacrifice.

Remember Maslow's hierarchy of needs? We're supposed to move *UP*! Once our primal safety, sustenance and shelter needs are taken care of – in the most basic way – our job, our *raison d'etre*, is to seek community, belonging, recognition, creative expression and self-actualization. Supporting clients to make that shift is something I love to do.

Jocelyn started our relationship trying to tell me that she didn't know what she wanted to do. Oh, that one again. Another story that, as a culture, it's really time we rewrote. Easily a full third of my clients start out telling me they don't know what they want to do and another third tell me they don't know somewhere in the middle. And the final third say they know what they want to do but they don't know how. When we're done our time together, though, no one ever *ends up* saying that, because it's simply not true, and it never was. We're born knowing what pleasure feels like. Ditto for attraction, reward, love, joy. And that inner knowing doesn't go away. It can just get obscured by the many layers of life we pile on top of it. And it can even be sitting right on top of the pile but we manage to look sideways or in fuzzy focus to avoid seeing it because we're afraid.

Just past her 40th birthday, Jocelyn had been working at a very boring job in a very boring law firm for a bloody boring long time. (Just to clarify, this is a case of different strokes for different folks. Some of my best friends are lawyers – really! – and I know it can be exciting and deeply satisfying work. In my next life I may even give it a try...) But to Jocelyn, all the files and contracts and triplicates and citations added up to an existence just this side of comatose. That's the "authentic you" part of this – it doesn't matter whether a lot of other people would say you have a great job. It only matters whether you feel like you're getting all you can out of your own unique experience of life.

By the time she came to see me, Jocelyn was 'working' 80 or more hours per week. Any of you with experience in legal cultures and law firms know that junior associates who someday wish to make partner are expected to bill a minimum of 50 hours per week, many even 60 or more. To bill 50, chances are that associate has to work 65 because not all hours worked are billable (administrative time; complimentary consultations; internal meetings; staff supervision, etc.) Jocelyn actually worked for a fairly enlightened firm and 50 billable hours a week would have made everyone happy and ensured that she advanced in the organization. But Jocelyn couldn't work 60 to bill 50. The way she had come to feel about her work, she simply couldn't focus any longer. It took her 80 – 90 hours per week to bill her below-average 45 because her mind was constantly wandering off, delving into fantasies of other lives and other places, anywhere but here. She longed to be some*place* else so she naturally was drawn to fantasies of being some*one* else. She knew she was in trouble the day that she came in to work on a Monday morning and learned that one of her colleagues had been rushed in for emergency surgery over the weekend and would be unable to work for several weeks. Jocelyn's response? *Envy.*

She called me on Tuesday.

Something in her voice said I should make time to see her as soon as possible, so on Wednesday she arrived before me saying, "I don't know what I want but it's not this. And it's definitely not being the kind of person who is jealous of someone being injured! That's awful! Who thinks such a thing?"

"More people than you think," I replied, and reassured her that no one thought she wanted her friend to be unwell, or that she herself wanted to be injured, only that her unconscious desire was telling her that she really needed a break. And while we were on the subject, I invited her to reframe her thoughts of wanting to "*be* someone else," and to instead consider that because *she is*, in fact, someone else – someone other than a law associate – she is naturally not adapting well to an environment that is not her own. Further, I suggested, considering she is not in her natural habitat, she's actually done very well and could give herself some credit for that. Starting from acceptance and gratitude pretty much always makes things go faster. And smoother. And end up better, too.

"Oh," said Jocelyn. "That's not what I would have thought at all. But it sounds logical enough that it could be true." The ability to go along with a rational idea that you can't quite believe in your vulnerable state but instinct says will support you can help you a long way in times like these. It would be a while before Jocelyn could experience herself as a strong, capable, creative and satisfied person who knew what she wanted for herself and didn't need to feel bad that she didn't want to be a successful corporate lawyer. But I did experience her that way, right from the start, and she was willing to go along with my experience while she sorted out her own – and that gave us all the tools we needed to get down to work.

We did some values clarification and journaling of favourite, most authentic moments Jocelyn had experienced in her young life. I also asked her to spend a day in the biography section of the bookstore, dipping into as many life stories as she could, and taking note of which ones excited her, which felt familiar, and which repelled and to make time each weekend to go somewhere new – not necessarily far afield, just a neighbourhood or park or beach where she hasn't been in a long time and to concentrate on really experiencing it. She needed to get her emotions, synapses and intuition firing. A half dozen sessions later, Jocelyn came in *beaming*. Literally! Her face was full of light and I knew she had found what she wanted.

"Well?" I said, smiling back at her. "Who are you?"

"I'm a travel writer. I use my gifts for language and observation and looking out for people's interests in strange and unusual circumstances [all skills she had honed as a lawyer, by the way] to let people relax, have a good time, and either live the adventure I lived by using my book as a guide or just have a getaway in their minds by reading the journey and opening up to another way of living [ah, also honouring what used to be her escape strategy at work, when she couldn't be a lawyer anymore]. I go all over the world and I meet amazing people and no two days are exactly alike. I'm ready to quit my job!" she finished breathlessly.

Bless her. Jocelyn was in for the ride of her life.

One of the most important lessons I've learned over the years of doing this work is the mission critical status I need to give to setting my client's expectations. Of course that includes a transparent discussion of their objectives and my expertise and the parameters of our work process. Much more than that, though, it's about making sure they know the ride they will be taking if they choose to take action and make the changes they have been dreaming about passively for so long.

When so much energy and urgency has built up over months or years and it is finally released, there is a very big burst, as you can well imagine (picture a car suddenly popping out of neutral and into drive when you've been gunning the gas, or taking the cap off a bottle of pop you've been shaking.) It's startling, explosive, exciting... and messy, hard to control and usually more than a little scary until you figure out what's going on.

So I always take care to talk to clients well in advance of reaching this stage about the 'halo effect' of the first big decision, when it feels like you have just fallen in love and won the lottery on the same day, and about the likely if not inevitable dip in energy that comes soon after. The lasting good news is, you've raised your baseline in taking a bold step in the direction of your self, thus even a dip still has you several notches above where you were when you felt all the urgency to change. The temporary bad news is that there may be quite a few ups and downs between where you are and where you seek to be.

I often turn to the (admittedly overused) metaphor of the roller coaster when I seek to prepare clients for the journey ahead. And my experience of roller coasters has without exception involved a point on the steep uphill climb when I see how far off the ground I am and before I go careening into some hairpin, upside-down, blood-curdling curve, when I would absolutely have gotten the @#*% off had the car magically slowed and a nice attendant come along to extend his hand to those of us having overwhelming second thoughts. This is usually, of course, also the point at which I begin screaming and promising myself that if I live through this, I will never, ever, under any circumstances, ever do it again. At that point in the ride, the excitement is all fear – desire erased from memory, the exhilaration that will come in 1.5 seconds too far off to even imagine.

The only way to get the desire and the exhilaration back is to take the whole ride to the end – which is why (in addition to safety and liability issues, of course), roller coasters strap you in on the ground and don't give you the option of getting off until the ride is back in the station. My job, when clients are where Jocelyn found herself, is to be the emotionally stabilizing equivalent of that strap, getting them to stay onboard to take the whole ride.

Right after the exhilaration of giving notice at her firm and putting her condo up for sale, right about the time that other associates starting coming by her office to pick up the files they would take over and she was getting kicked out of her place for entire weekends while the realtor held open houses, yup, right about the time that her life felt completely inverted and she had no idea which way was up, Jocelyn began to scream just as if she were on the "Twister" or the "Cyclone" or whatever those rides are being called these days. She wanted to tell her managing partner that she's made a mistake and would take the such-and-such file back. She wanted to throw the looky-loos off her 17th floor balcony. And she wanted me to tell her what to do next.

> I'm a big believer in strategic planning but the first component of the plan for me is always to find the leverage, the thing you do that will give you more energy to do the other things you need to do. And nine times out of ten, that leverage is love.

Fortunately, Jocelyn was strapped in. She knew this experience was probably coming and knew to call me when she started freaking out so we could talk her back into herself. And it was actually pretty easy. She'd panic, call me, talk for a few minutes, recommit to her plan, have another anxiety attack, come in to talk, calm down, refocus, lose it a little again, send me an email, remember who she was and what she wanted, then forget again and call me... and in that rhythm Jocelyn got through her last month on the job, handing over her clients, (almost) enjoying the cake and balloons at her firm's going-away party for her, and readying herself to put her things in storage and GO SOMEWHERE!

Jocelyn began researching all of the magazines, online communities, tv production companies and guidebook publishers who might accept her stories. She read back issues of "The Writers Market" and immersed herself in an online journalism course. She spoke with a few freelance writers, and began working on a budget for what she would need to live on while she worked on proposals and pitches to get her first overseas writing gig. All very logical, linear, strategic action steps... and so very much in the wrong direction!

I knew that Jocelyn would lose steam this way: she was thinking like a lawyer, not like a creative. I'm a big believer in strategic planning but the first component of the plan for me is always to find the leverage, the thing you do that will give you more energy to do the other things you need to do. And nine times out of ten, that leverage is love. Jocelyn didn't love the research. She didn't love footnotes, documentation, MLA and Turabian formats for quoting and margins. She certainly didn't love budgets. Those are the things she would be willing to do for love of satisfying work – even do them happily with enough joy in the work itself – but on their own? She may just as well have been sourcing clauses for a shareholder agreement for all the joy she felt. Yet every time I tried to nudge her over to dreaming, she kept saying "Yeah, yeah, I just need to do this first."

Okay, so the roller coaster takes another dip. We can handle it. We know what to expect. And when Jocelyn came into my office with a spreadsheet and a deep sadness on her face, I knew she was ready to hear me this time.

"All the magazines say they need to see an article before they would be willing to consider me for an assignment. And most of the writers I met say freelancing is a really hard life. There's no stability. You have to work really hard," Jocelyn lamented.

"Okay," I said. "But you know you can write an article, right?"

"Yeah, but..." Jocelyn started.

"Hang on – simple question. Can you do it?"

"Yes."

"Okay, and you've already had 'stable,' in your life, right? You had 80 hours a week of stable and didn't want it, so that was never the goal of our work, was it?"

"No."

"Okay, so we don't have to worry about irrelevant information. What about the hard work part? Do you think if you were sitting at a table beside some Greek ruins right now, clicking away on your laptop, writing a story about some schoolchildren who are putting on a play with new a modern myth of Demeter and Zeus, that you would care how long it took to write? Would it seem like the work was too hard?"

"No."

"Any more problems up your sleeve?" I asked as Jocelyn grinned and shook her head.

"Okay, so let's try this the right way, by doing what you love first and figuring out the rest after that. Write something. This week. Be a tourist within driving distance of home, find a story, and write it. Bring me 1500 words next week."

And she did. For three weeks, Jocelyn wrote a different story each week. She kept asking if there was any other homework and I kept saying no. The work is *the work*. Love it, do it, trust it, *be* it. And when she brought in her third story, she said she'd had a realization. (No surprise there – they always come if we make space for them.)

Jocelyn realized that she couldn't really write more than about three or four hours a day, anyway. After four hours, her productivity really went down and she didn't like it as much. She wanted her main thing, her purpose, to be writing, but she could see herself doing other things as well. Maybe if she could find some other work in a place she would like to write about, she would be able to support herself while she did her writing and have stories to use to introduce herself to publishers.

Ureeka! We quickly rejected the idea of her shopping her legal skills around – she felt like that chapter in her life needed to be closed, at least for a few years. I mentioned a client of mine who was teaching in an English Language school in Korea and liking it very much because he was only in the classroom five hours per day, four days a week, and had three weeks off between each trimester to travel around Asia. Jocelyn got that beaming look again...

A few dozen emails and photo exchanges and phone calls and visa applications later, and Jocelyn had joined my other client at the same school. She taught there for two years, all the while traveling in the region, writing and publishing several articles. In her third year she transferred to a school in China and started writing for some online communities focused on the expatriate teaching experience. And last I heard she was looking for a placement in South America, ready to experience another language and culture from the inside out, and starting up a blog. Once she got creative enough, she began to realize she didn't need to wait for an assignment to publish and share her talent with the world.

And the joyfully creative roller coaster ride continues. . .

And so to Andre's ride: equally creative, joyful and up and down and up again. Andre's experience was one of knowing he was an artist, making his living as an artist, and, sadly, finding that the making of the living was taking all the art out of it. Too often the experience of commodifying the artistic work saps its creativity – or, more significantly, saps the creativity of the artist.

Andre and I began working together shortly after his 54th birthday, when he left his career as a chef but before he had determined what would follow. In his words, "Twelve years of late nights, less than desirable working conditions and long hours standing on my feet had taken their toll and I knew my life had to be different or soon it wouldn't be a life at all. I still loved food, still had a passion for creating new dishes, but I had already come to hate preparing a lot of them for restaurant guests who had no idea what went into it. And I knew I had to leave before I began to hate all of it." Andre was very wise to heed his own signals and move quickly. It was definitely time for change... more, different, less, better... what? That's the part he (thought he) didn't know. By now *you* know better than that, though, don't you?

One of the very first exercises I asked Andre to try after I got to know him and we had worked through an intake assessment process was a present-tense journaling of his no-holds-barred ideal day. Lots of coaches use this type of exercise because the capacity of detailed narrative to sweep us away and thus to sweep away our resistance can help us arrive at a clarity of passion and purpose which direct questioning rarely achieves. Guided visualization and directed dreaming can also accomplish this goal very well. In narrative, for me it's all about the *minutiae*: love is in the details, as they say. We may not always know what we want to do for a living, but we always know, when we give ourselves permission to dream, how we want to live.

Andre's narrative was *beautiful*! It was full of passion for food and people, for beautiful spaces and service to others. But mostly it was beautifully written. Believe me, writers know other writers when we meet them on a page. It's a tribal kind of recognition. It was immediately clear to us both that, somehow, using his gift for writing *in tandem* with his loves of good food and helping people was his path. A cookbook was a natural first consideration – but because it was also scary and initially too big and vague an idea, it was equally natural to "delay" it. "The world doesn't need another cookbook," came Fear's first argument; then "It would have to be a really, really good cookbook or there'd be no point." Uh huh. Another two weeks of exploring other options before: "If it turns out to be a good book, I'm going to have to go on TV to promote it and I don't have anything to wear." Seriously? *That* was his story?! This (il)logic ran its course and, fortunately, after a period of bringing the rest of his life into alignment (organizing his home, improving his morning fitness regimen, catching up with some old friends, painting his den and adding some additional RAM to his computer, etc.), Andre became open to really embracing his idea.

Even then, we did some back and forth. Andre would let himself get caught up in an idea for a particular recipe, a story to open some section on the romance of food, and then he would think to himself "I don't know how to do that," and his aspirations would come thudding to the ground. He would become convinced it was nothing but a pipedream. And I would tell him as I am telling you now: every success starts with a plan and every plan starts as a pipedream. Even the most strategic minds in the world don't know *all* the steps they will take before they take them, and many don't know any at all. They choose to be open to finding out, to set as the primary intention of their being the truth of Peter Block's great line: "The answer to How? is Yes."

They say that once a student is ready, a teacher will appear. I also believe that once the authentic self is ready, an opportunity will appear. When Andre said Yes! to himself, the universe said Yes! back to him. Very soon after arriving at a place where he was able to say, "I'm not sure if it's the best career or business decision or not, but I *want* to write a cookbook," serendipity arrived to do its part and Andre learned of a cookbook writing course about to be taught in just two weeks' time by a highly respected food writer. With one discovery – and its companion, a leap of faith – Andre found his vision. He says, "The course taught me a few important things: first, there is an almost inexhaustible market for cookbooks and even the bad ones get published. I also realized that there are no truly original ideas, even in the good cookbooks. Every idea for a recipe comes from somewhere else and is tweaked and refined into a new version. In fact, every time I cook, I am creating new recipes. But the most important knowledge I gained, through contact with and encouragement from our excellent instructor was that I did, in fact, have a very strong and well developed food sensibility, some pretty good ideas, and the ability to communicate those ideas well."

Born of a natural gift, cultivated by self awareness and nurtured with equal parts mustered courage and acceptance of support and encouragement, the vision emerged: Andre would write a cookbook which married his love of our Pacific Northwest place in the world with his gift for creating elegant tapas using organic ingredients and fused from a variety of cultures.

Andre's action plan began as a mix of general direction and specific timelines. Why? Because timelines have a way of helping general ideas to become more specific like nothing else can. Without structure – deadlines being their ultimate form – it's much harder for most of us to achieve. With structure, we're paradoxically freer to create (rather than just creatively procrastinating). That's why I set an absolute 30-day time limit on each client getting started into motion, in however small a way that might be. Because there's no substitute for action – and nothing prepares you for action like action itself.

So, Andre's general direction involved three basic actions, each subsequently broken down into little steps:

1. Clarify genre of cookbook as much as possible within timeline
2. Begin research into other cookbooks, cooking magazines, and resources on food writing for guidance
3. Develop a preliminary time map starting with 20 hours of work on cookbook each week

His specific timeline was, you guessed it, 30 days.

Notice the key words and phrases in each planning step: begin, as much as possible, preliminary, starting with. Any good plan for first actions has to acknowledge that you are a beginner at the beginning. The desire to have everything all sorted out and know exactly where you are headed can hold you up much more substantially than even failing to plan at all (thought I wouldn't recommend that either!) The only thing you can know for sure is that you've got to get started. Neither completely ready nor set (because you never will be), you still GO!

After gathering together several hundred recipe ideas as part of his planning and strategy, the time came for Andre to begin to develop and test them as a prelude to writing. His time map called for shopping for one or two hours each morning, then cooking and making notes for four to six hours as necessary – three days each week – choosing recipes based on which ingredients were in season locally at the moment. Each week's specific plan was recorded in his PDA for structure. For example, a typical weekday looked something liked this:

7am	- Meditate
	- Read
	- Shower
	- Dress
8am	- Review schedule and recipes over breakfast
	- Check supply of staples
	- Prepare and clean kitchen
	- Go to market to buy saffron, prawns, mussels and clams for paella
10am	- Start cooking!
	- Remember to take careful notes on quantities, weights, oven temperatures and specific methods used
1pm	- Break
4pm	- Have make-ahead items complete & prep done forlast-minute cooking

6pm   - Set up kitchen for dinner prep and dining room for
arrival of guests

7pm   - Serve dinner and solicit feedback

9pm   - Clean-up
- Decide whether recipe was a success, a failure or needs
re-testing

This was a great starting place for that all-important first week, during which Andre was reminded that he can become so involved in what he's doing when he cooks that he can lose track of just about everything else. Good for the soul, but not so great for the record-keeping process that would yield replicable recipes. Over the next few weeks, Andre refined his plan to include use of more precise measuring tools and a custom-made recipe testing form to make it easier for him to track and record method and variations.

After getting so involved in the testing of recipes for one kind of berry that he missed his window on the purchase of another kind of berry from his favourite local supplier of organics, Andre developed a much more detailed master schedule which accounted for growing seasons with greater precision. When memory failed to reconstruct his cooking process to his satisfaction more than a few days after recipe testing, Andre changed his schedule to alternate cooking days with writing days so that experiences and ideas are as fresh in his mind as the ingredients in his food. (Sorry, I couldn't resist a little more food-inspired wordplay! I got to taste some of those test meals, too. As the daughter of a very talented chef, I sold my culinary skills as much as my coaching ones to get a seat at Andre's wonderful table... I often say my work with clients is a delicious joy: this time it was just so much more than the metaphor!)

Today, Andre's plan is well-refined and he is living the life of a cookbook writer. He cooks and tests two to three recipes each on Tuesdays and Thursdays, and writes up completed recipes, with great anecdotes and headnotes to go with them, on Wednesdays and Fridays. On writing days Andre also revisits his overall timeline, schedules re-testings and makes time for editing. Because motivation can be a challenge to maintain on a consistent basis even when you love your work, Andre and I developed a structural tool which serves his very well over the long term: at the beginning of each month, he emails "Test Dinner Menus" with a guest sign-up sheet to family and friends. He is *publicly* committed to following through on his testing schedule and you just know he'll reach his goals. People will be showing up to eat!

Also of interest is the way that some of the "headnotes" for certain recipes have grown well beyond the bounds of the cookbook genre and become stories in their own right, some of them already published as travel writing or anecdotes on a restaurant website. Andre's gifts are growing because he is giving them a loving, creative space in his life to find their way. There's no question that Andre's cookbook will be completed; it's only a matter of when, and he has a schedule for that. More books will inevitably follow. He simply *is* a writer: not by virtue of publication, but by virtue of opening to a vision of himself and then living that vision.

Writing, art, music, film, interior design, gardening, dance, cooking… dreaming and living in creative ways. Such beautiful examples of love made visible, don't you think? Whatever you see as your career path, ask yourself each day what you can do to let your inner artist come out and play. There is an artist in all of us, just waiting to be fabulous.

Chapter 3

Fast Tracks:

Type A Overachievers and Work/Life in the C-Suite

Ah, the fast track. This is the high octane, adrenaline-charged road most people assume I travel every day, thinking that leadership coaching and career management is exclusive to executives and CEO wannabes. Certainly my practice has plenty of high achieving professionals in a wide range of fields including senior corporate officers, but the common denominator is a desire to live fully and well, with career given a prominent but not necessarily first (or even second or third) place in a highly individualized conception of work/life which centres on, you guessed it: expressing love and actualizing self, even if few might have used that vocabulary at first.

What makes a career truly rich is the way that it creates a meaningful context for self expression – that beautiful love made visible – in tandem with the way it lays a foundation for so many other wonderful gifts in life. I often say, whether speaking about my work in career management, recruitment or employee engagement consulting, that I don't have a target demographic. Rather, I have an attractive psychographic (lucky me!), made up of people who want to *love* their work/life, and who share a desire to live in an authentic and values-driven way, even if those values may differ from person to person, company to company.

The stories which follow here are indeed about a fast track: these talented and assertive clients moved quickly to places of prominence in their organizations and enjoyed the rewards which accompany that progress. Neither, however, even cursory observation will reveal, saw the promotion or the compensation plan as an end or even a reward in itself: their motives, their paths, and their results are much deeper and more abundant than anything which can be reduced to a name plate or a pay stub, and their stories are highly instructive for anyone out there who has their sights set "higher" and is "wanting more." Dare to dream; dare even more to be *specific* in your intention because you can and will create what you believe you will create.

Rebecca, an extremely bright 34 year-old woman, came to me when she was newly wed and newly relocated with her husband to my home city of Vancouver, Canada. She had held two Director level jobs in New York and Toronto before love – and an increasing sense that a sea-to-sky rather than city-that-never-sleeps approach to life might suit her better – brought her to the Pacific Coast. Despite her professed openness to the west coast lifestyle and happiness to be here, Rebecca was clearly suffering from culture shock, both as a new bride in a new city away from her family, longtime friends and all things familiar to her, and as someone used to knocking back three espressos before her first morning meeting was over suddenly finding herself in a world where Starbucks sells more green tea and chai than lattes or cappuccino. (I'm exaggerating, of course, but this is about what Rebecca was *feeling*, not about objective statistics on caffeine consumption, so let's just play along, okay?)

Rebecca came in flustered and trying to hide it, then just letting it all hang out over the course of our first meeting. "You've got my resume, right?" Rebecca checked. "So you know I've held progressively responsible positions over the past ten years. Had I stayed in Toronto, I would have made VP within the next 18 months. Please bear in mind that's not hubris; it's just the track I was on. Then Chad came along and, well, you know how that is. Once we decided to get engaged, working 80 hour weeks didn't make sense anymore, not for me or for him. He had the opportunity to take a transfer out here – he's already a VP – and we both thought that the lifestyle we could enjoy in Vancouver would be better for us and for starting a family in a year or two."

"So my thing is," she continued, barely pausing to breathe, "I want to get my career on track as quickly as possible so I'll be in a good place to take that maternity leave, spend some time with my children when they're small, and have something solid to come back to. I don't have what it takes to be a stay-at-home mom forever, and I don't think I need to. We have so many more options now. I want to be happy and fulfilled in my own life and help my children feel the same way about their lives. I don't think that's too much to ask. It doesn't have to be a VP role, but obviously that's the direction I'm headed in. VP, Marketing, that is."

There was an ever-so-brief pause for me to I say, "Ye-es…"

"You know, the thing is that Vancouver has been a real surprise," Rebecca muses. "Not just the rain. I mean, people tell you about that. And the people in sandals and bicycle shorts and yoga pants everywhere. Even in the rain. It's so funny. But that's not it, either. It's the *laissez faire-ness* of the whole place. Everyone is so 'let's take it easy.' And it seems like most people here are not very career-oriented. Then again, I guess if that were true, you wouldn't have such a big practice and you clearly do so maybe I got that wrong. I hope that didn't offend you. I'm sure you work with a lot of very driven people, or people who think they have drive. And I'm sure you have drive yourself, of course."

I smile and say, "Well, uh…"

"Not that I mean there is anything wrong with Vancouver," Rebecca quickly reasserted. I love it here. I'm glad we came. It's just taking some getting used to because it seems like there are no real decision-makers here. Not that they aren't real, you understand, just that it seems like money decisions, marketing decisions, the C-level stuff, well it can't happen here because there are no – or hardly any – C-level people here. Regional offices not head offices. Or not as many as I am used to, anyway. But we really like it. Chad has a really good job. And the ocean is so beautiful – we walk the seawall every weekend. When he has a day off. So do you think I can get a VP level job in a few months? I don't expect it to be right, right away, although that would be ideal, but soon, you know? Soon. Am I being realistic?"

I'd like to be able to tell you that I answered Rebecca's question. But actually the "dialogue" went on as transcribed above for at least another thirty minutes before I was able to utter more than monosyllabic replies. (And as you can gather from my verbosity throughout the overall narrative of this book, it takes a special kind of talker to keep me quiet for so long...) Despite her out-of-control speech – or maybe even a little because of it – I liked Rebecca a lot. Smart, engaged, and high octane are qualities I relate to. And yet I knew I wasn't seeing anything close to her best self.

Rebecca was on what I sometimes call 'crash overload.' She was used to mustering up and expending a certain amount and intensity of energy every day. She was accustomed to planning, focus, accomplishment, and direction and she had very little of any of those on this day. Her world revolved around a certain pace of work and life and a certain amount of social contact. Suddenly all of the contexts changed and she was nowhere near caught up. So she was still manufacturing all that energy but had nowhere to put it: hence 'crash overwhelm.' Great truths are found in paradox, yes?

So *aaaallll* of Rebecca's pent-up and suddenly excess energy came tumbling out in my office. This experience is not unique to executives or even particularly high achievers of other stripes. I've seen it with a lot of people at all levels in a wide variety of fields. What they have in common is that they have been unemployed and without adequate social structure for several weeks or months before they see me. They've had far too many hours alone with their heads spinning about the situation they are in and the changes they are facing, and they feel a quite desperate need to share those thoughts. Heck, I've been there myself and I'm sure many of you reading can relate, too.

Yet, as must be obvious, I can't begin to do my job until clients in this overwhelmed and overwhelming state release some of that swirling energy, so I serve as the outlet for awhile. Go ahead, dump it all here! Vancouver Rebecca would eventually settle in just fine; but first Toronto/New York Rebecca had to be willing to let go and take the ride.

> I'm a big fan of speed. I think our culture over-emphasizes patience as a way of rationalizing our fears about our desires and our power to create them. I believe that when we are focused, clear and intentional, we can make great leaps toward our desires in a fluid, organic, graceful and even transformative way.

At the end of that first meeting, I asked Rebecca to go to the public library and the local volunteer connections agency to speak with people about Vancouver companies with more than 100 staff, whether head or regional offices, and to gather information on organizations needing fundraising or board level community service. These labour-intensive and high contact research tasks would, I knew, help burn off some more energy and have the side benefit of restoring some of Rebecca's sense of social grace as she got back in the habit of talking *with* people instead of pouring herself out on them.

Not surprisingly, Rebecca came in the following week with a fifteen page spreadsheet itemizing and cross-referencing all of the opportunities she had identified, and she immediately wanted an attack strategy to land a job with one of the companies *now*, then see which charity work might be able to fit in to her schedule after she had secured employment.

I'm a big fan of speed. I think our culture over-emphasizes patience as a way of rationalizing our fears about our desires and our power to create them. I believe that when we are focused, clear and intentional, we can make great leaps toward our desires in a fluid, organic, graceful and even transformative way.

I also knew that Rebecca wasn't feeling anywhere near focused, clear or intentional yet, so speed could not be her friend that day. She was feeling desperate and fearful, and that is a place from which we attract proof that things are as hard as we think they are, not the joyful outcomes we desire. My desire, then, was to support her to slow down briefly enough to achieve the state of consciousness she would need to enjoy the fast track the way I knew she wanted to and could enjoy it. That news, as you can perhaps imagine, did not go over big in the first instance.

"You want me to *what?*" Rebecca said when I suggested that we do some reflection, writing, imagery, affirmations and a vision board to help her reach clarity about her ideal career and belief in her ability to bring it to life. "I didn't come here for therapy. I'm good at what I do and I just need you to help me make the right connections to find a good company to do it in. Aren't we going to work on my resume? Set up some interviews?"

I assured her that resumes and interviews would be important tools on this journey, but first we needed a destination. "You don't just want a job; nobody hires someone like me just to get a job," I said.

"Of course not. I want my career back," Rebecca sharply interjected.

"Well, I'm not sure I entirely believe you," I replied gently, trying to create some space with my voice for what I needed to say next, to help Rebecca open to hearing it. She started to answer but then relaxed her body a little and looked at me expectantly, at once suspicious and curious, a workable emotional state for a new beginning.

"You started out telling me about the shift you felt when you met Chad, about a desire for a more 'west coast' kind of life, about wanting to feel more fulfilled in your work and have more balance to blend a family with your career, remember? And you came to see *me*, the 'live your values,' 'take your soul to work' specialist. The internet and yellow pages are full of resume writing services and people who claim 30 and 60 day executive placement. You could have signed on for a more transactional service if you wanted, but you picked *me*. So, by what you have said, and by the intention you have expressed in your actions, I believe you want something more. What do you believe?"

Rebecca looked at me for a long time. Then she checked out my carpet for awhile. Then she picked up a pen and her notebook and doodled for a minute or two. This was one of those times when patience was exactly what was needed, and I needed to discipline my own energy to hold space for her to tap into her voice. At last, she said "You might have guessed I'm a pretty good multi-tasker." (I grinned.) "Can I do your values exercises and get to work on my resume at the same time?"

I said I wouldn't have it any other way.

We first selected a few charities where Rebecca could immediately start doing some volunteer work: she would meet people, remind herself what she is good at, and get into the flow of community life in her new city: all critical to her energy, mood and ability to attract what she wanted. Concurrent with that work, I asked her to go to a really good newsstand or bookstore – the kind with seventeen racks of specialty magazines you've never heard of – and buy five or six of them that look 'strangely appealing,' that "I'm-drawn-to-this-but-don't-know-why" sensation that lets us know our subconscious has something to tell us. From those magazines, Rebecca pulled images and built a vision board collage, then journaled her response to it. The images, we both noted, focused a great deal on teamwork, play and nature. Hmmm.

We then spent some time going over the companies to which Rebecca felt the most drawn from her research. I didn't care about financial profiles or marketing mix at this point. There would be plenty of time to strategically analyze the right career move once we had found the kinds of organizations that attracted her. I wanted to know, on a visceral level, what just *clicked*.

It took a few stabs at this to get there, as Rebecca kept wanting to talk about who had a posting or which companies appeared to be best positioned for aggressive growth. When she at last identified some companies she had simply gotten excited about, she was squashing her exuberance before even feeling it by rushing to reasons why a given company was a bad idea – too small, no executive opportunity, too unfamiliar, not enough money in the industry. I encouraged her to put those kinds of worries aside for a moment and just consider what she was drawn to in these organizations. I invited her to realize that she was far too smart and capable to make a rash decision, thus she could afford to let her mind take a backseat for just this initial filtering process and let her heart guide her. Eventually, Rebecca was able to apply our pure attraction, 'no criteria criterion' to a selection of three companies for discussion.

Company A's website, Rebecca said, used so much language that resonated for her. "They didn't just talk about quality and service in some vague way like so many organizations do. They had a whole page about loyalty, filled with testimonials from clients who had been with them for many years. And I saw a few of their sample ads, and they were saying thank you for the business they had received over the years, thank you for trusting us. That kind of thing can be hokey, or obviously disingenuous. Even the exact same words and layout could feel contrived, and I have a pretty low threshold for that, given my marketing background and the amount of spin I've seen and done. But for some reason, I liked this," Rebecca concluded.

And I liked where Rebecca was letting herself go: "I don't know why but I completely believe X" is a great testament to the strength of the attraction and the heart-connection behind it. Intuition, higher self, gut instinct, nagging sense, subconscious message… whatever you want to call "it," we know it when we feel it. And it's a good place from which to lead a search for direction.

Rebecca continued with her thoughts on Companies B and C. "B is working in manufacturing, and I've done a lot of that. I don't really know anything about their product, and their branding was frankly pretty low-end, but I really liked what I read about their systems, and the way they actually make the product. I felt like I wanted to help them leverage their systems better to make that part of their brand. Isn't that interesting? I don't think I even knew that was how I was responding until I said it!" Yes, interesting indeed. And Company C? "I'm not even completely sure what they do. I followed a link from a job posting to their Careers page and they had all these pictures of their staff and some stories of people who had been working for them for several years. I feel silly saying it, but this is what you want me to do, right? This is your thing! They looked like great people I would want to know. So there!"

I had to laugh. And what a great thing to be able to say – my work regularly and richly inspires laughter! Precisely why I completely understand that Rebecca would be drawn to a company populated by people she senses she would want to know. That's who my clients are to me, and that's why I do what I do. So, yeah, that's my thing, and I was very happy for Rebecca's heart-based discoveries.

From there we went into some values work, identifying the core values Rebecca would seek to live out as follows, in order of highest importance:

1. Love & Connection
2. Creativity
3. Excellence
4. Family/Work Balance
5. Challenge & Intensity
6. Recognition & Financial Reward
7. Beauty & Aesthetics
8. Collaborative Teamwork

An interesting mix, don't you think? A little of a fairly wide variety of things, and many of them already well-evidenced in what we have learned about Rebecca. We spent quite a bit of time talking about how these values had been expressed in her life so far, how she would ideally like to see them expressed, and to what degree and in what ways she felt they needed to be part of just her career versus her life as a whole. Like many people ready for an integrated and authentic work/life experience, the powerful slash linking them instead of a gap separating them, Rebecca concluded that the only job which would be right for her would give regular expression to *all* of her values. She was looking for the full meal deal, and feeling more confident with each day that we focused on what she cared about that she could have it.

We inventoried her skills and experience, crafted a professional profile which reflected both the values she cared about and the value she could deliver to the right organization, and put together two versions of her resume: a one page, slickly formatted 'teaser' that befit her role in marketing, and another more exhaustive version, closer to a CV, though still very achievement- and results-oriented. We then turned our efforts to relationship-building in and around the kinds of organizations which could be a fit for her. She began sending letters of introduction, making follow-up calls and making the rounds of breakfast, luncheon, coffee and even cocktail meetings with people working in and around the companies to which she had felt the greatest 'pull.'

Rebecca naturally wanted to take a straight shot at her chosen targets but I persuaded her to bide her time, freshen up her networking

> You always know you are on the right track when your vision creates a win on all levels and for all parties....Even if you don't get everything you would choose all in one step, what you do get will feel intact and whole and have the capacity to grow organically to the next level.

and relationship-building skills, get comfortable in her own skin in this new environment, and learn more about these industries and organizations before she attempted a full frontal assault.

The time proved to be an excellent investment: Rebecca learned that she knew some of the same people as one of the Directors in Company A and, with a few simple calls, she could have a personal introduction. She learned the ins and outs of the systems and protocols at Company B and could bring that knowledge into a meeting or interview. And most significantly she found the confidence and centre of her inner executive again: no more compulsive disclosure or 'crash overwhelm.' Practiced, polished and feeling equally passionate and composed, Rebecca was ready to put her intention into action.

More letters and phone calls, this time with introductions and referrals to give them a boost, begat several meetings with key players in all three companies, and eventually to second- and third-level meetings in Company B. Rebecca's research and relationship-building allowed her to propose a number of key ideas that the Company could use to make its local manufacturing and use of many sustainable materials as much more of a competitive advantage in its branding and positioning, competing on quality and ethos instead of speed and price: they were interested and enthusiastic and Rebecca was ecstatic. (Suddenly the teams-working-in-nature photos she had so loved made sense...) But when the offer came, at only a Manager level title and salary at $75,000 per year, $20,000 lower than her most recent base, she was crestfallen.

Ah, time for me to remind her that all things are negotiable...

"Forget the terms of the offer for a moment," I urged. "Let's focus on what really matters. Under the right terms, just taking the details as a given, do you genuinely want to work for this company? Do you trust these people? Do you see a future in this industry? Are you excited about what your role could be, what you would learn, how you would grow? Are you just head over heels in love with the possibilities this job could bring?"

Yes on every count came the answers. "Then I think you should make it work for you," I said. "But I don't want to settle," came Rebecca's reply. "Not settling. Never settling. When have you *ever* heard me say that? Perish the thought. Making it work. Setting the intention and creating it," is what I replied.

Any good sales person knows that when there is buy-in at the level of emotion and principle, the details can easily be worked out with some creativity and openness on both sides. Rebecca and I used what she had learned from her very careful research around and within the company – and what I have learned about inspiring employers to stretch their systems a little to engage good people – and together we put together a proposal for a staggered entry to the company.

We very carefully considered all of the company's known and intuited objectives and needs in equal measure alongside her own, and built a concrete and practical proposal that was compellingly persuasive. She would have the title of Director and base of $75K for a probationary period of three months with set project deliverables which, if met, would increase her compensation to $85K until the end of her first year when, again if deliverables were met with respect to some strategic partnerships and the relationship between marketing and sales, her base compensation would increase to $95K with the option of another $15K-$20K in profit sharing.

At the end of year two, a solid performance review would secure Rebecca the title of Vice President, another bump in salary and uncapped profit sharing based on performance. We would get her to a VP level in only six months more time than she had estimated she would have reached it had she stayed in her previous job, and add to the mix a higher salary, and living with a man she loved in the city she had chosen. Not a bad day's work, I'd say.

You always know you are on the right track when your vision creates a win on all levels and for all parties. I believe that the psychology of compromise, of looking for what can be chipped away in trade-offs rather than built up to abundantly ensure everyone's desires are met, can only diminish experience. You can't create a whole product out of a piecemeal process; the whole can be greater than the sum of its parts only when all of the parts are honest, loving, generative, optimistic... Start with second choices, concessions, takeaways and diversionary tactics and anything you do manage to build will be misshapen and unsatisfying.

Believe in what you actually want; trust yourself; then actualize your dream and your self in the process. Even if you don't get everything you would choose all in one step, what you do get will feel intact and whole and have the capacity to grow organically to the next level. That's what this staggered advancement plan was transparently built to do.

It took some explaining and two meetings' worth of back and forth about the metrics used to evaluate her performance milestones, but Rebecca's eventual contract reflected the terms as above. Four years later, she is of course a VP. I understand her company's revenues are up by 20% over previous projections since she came on board and she is earning well over $140K per year. Rebecca also reports having at last learned to like herbal tea (just in time for giving up caffeine in pregnancy...) Love made visible again.

We might plan our lives around big, momentous decisions but, in the end, our lives are defined by the small choices we make every day.

Values-based living is only possible if we're prepared to engage in equally values-based energy, time and priority management. And for executives on the fast track, literally booking meetings and conference calls in ten-minute increments throughout 16 hour days, there are many more decisions and many more opportunities to confirm or be swayed from the values direction they have set.

Take the example of Max: the fifty-something CEO of a thriving and progressive private company in which all employees of more than two years' tenure, at every level in the organization, share in the distribution of 30% of the company's profits among them, and several enjoy stock options as well. You know in that description alone that he is already living some very important values. Max's powerful commitment to his company and his employees are matched only by his community involvement and spiritual connection, and his love for his family.

When we met, he was putting the kinds of pressures on himself that only the truly passionate, gifted and generous can: he was trying to value 30 or 40 people, passions and possibilities on any given day, stretching himself well past his breaking point, and losing satisfaction in all the things he once loved as his energy, mood, health, relationships and productivity progressively depleted. With each scramble to improve any one area, he damaged another. Dramatic change was needed or he feared he would lose the dream he had so lovingly built in his ten year-old company, to say nothing of his marriage and his health.

Like many of my clients, Max had come to me with an awareness that, even if our families or our health, community or spirituality rate as more important to us than career, by virtue of the time and energy we expend and the pervasive influences of culture and finance, work shapes our lives more than any other influence. A great marriage, however much we may appreciate it, is not something that carries us in a good mood throughout every workday if those workdays are really tough – the influence of the boss, the co-workers, the clients, traffic, suppliers, technology… is too much and too strong.

Conversely, a good day at work, many people I have coached report, can give them energy for their relationship, children and home-making. And almost nothing is more toxic to a family than a 'bad day' at work brought home, or the stresses and energy drains of major financial worries, so even a fulfilling personal life can be damaged, too often irreparably, by the wrong work experience.

Even a powerfully positive experience of career is no substitute for the other rich loves and comforts of life; career, however, is one of the great drivers of those other peak experiences, if we learn how to leverage it. More and more often my clients are coming to me referred by doctors, massage and physiotherapists, naturopaths, marriage counsellors, meditation teachers and clergy in recognition of the fact that, for many of them, the barrier or the stressor that is damaging their health, relationships or spiritual connection is the way they are going about their work. And so it was with Max.

Here is the snapshot with which we began: Max ran a business employing over 135 people. Family of five. Diagnosed with a major risk for heart attack or stroke. Experiencing a noticeable loss of joy and even simple affect such that all those intimate with Max were urging him to get some help. A scope so big is a major life project, one that had to be worked from the top down and the bottom up at the same time.

To make changes to the whole of his work/life, we first had to create space for even an hour or two a week to meet with me, let alone to do any homework or begin making significant conscious and systemic changes. Let me be clear: I wanted to help Max better create his work/life. To do that, I had to first help him better manage his energy. To do that, I first had to help him manage his time so we could get together! Sometimes we have to take a few steps backward in order to get the push-off we need to spring forward.

Like many leaders working well beyond a healthy capacity, Max believed he had no time to even think about how to get more time; he had a problem so bad it needed to be solved before he could work on a solution. It took him three weeks to schedule his first appointment with me and then he rescheduled the first attempt and outright cancelled the second. This was going to take some radical thinking.

"Let me talk directly to your assistant," I said. "Huh? That's a little overboard, I think!" came Max's first try at being open to change. "She doesn't need to be involved in this. She doesn't even know who you are. Let's see what we can do for next week."

"That's precisely my point, Max," I replied. "You're trying to do everything alone, denying the people who work with you and care for you the opportunity to get on board with helping you. It's your current consciousness that created this situation where you are so, forgive me, 'Maxed out.' You need a different consciousness to make change. And I can't help you get there if I can't even get into your calendar. So to make the first move, your assistant and I are going to be the consciousness. Later – very, very soon, I promise, you'll take over. Just give me permission to talk to her."

Max grumbled but he eventually introduced me to a lovely woman named Carol who had been managing his schedule for years. Problem was, as I suspected, that he would routinely add things to the schedule that she didn't know about and get himself double- and triple-booked, and he had created a culture in which his 'open door' policy had no boundaries. I'm big on flat hierarchies and transparent communication in the companies for which I consult. But I'm just as big on the organizational structure and personal boundaries necessary to give those relationships a chance to grow in a positive way.

So I talked with Carol about what Max would need: time zones setting out pre-planned leadership consultation time with his managers; community consultation time with the wider employee community; closed door CEO time for thinking, writing, and just being the guy who has the weight of it all on his shoulders; one 30 minute break for a walk or other exercise midday and 15 minute breaks every 90 minutes for transitioning, snacking and getting his focus back to turn his attention to the next thing, these essential elements of the Human Performance Institute's *Power of Full Engagement*[§] program.

He also needed two hours a week to meet with me and three additional hours for homework I would give him; and two hours a day of otherwise unscheduled flex time to handle the stuff that we all know is going to come up. And in Max's case, we'd stretch that to three hours until he got used to not scheduling *over* Carol's schedule or he'd never get that time for real. When people asked for an appointment, anything routine would get slotted into its pre-planned category; anything urgent would go into the built-in flex time.

[§] See Jim Loehr and Tony Schwartz, *The Power of Full Engagement: Managing Energy, Not Time, Is the Key to High Performance and Personal Renewal*. New York: Free Press, 2003.

The main problem that busy people have is that they over-commit and over-schedule and every minute of every day is already accounted for when the unplanned inevitably happens and sends them into a panic of shuffling and shunting tasks and appointments from which they never fully recover, sapping much-needed energy. So we were going to make sure Max had a buffer. Carol wasn't sure she understood all of it right away, but we mapped it and colour-coded it and checked in with each other daily as she was first scheduling him in this way, and together we worked the kinks out. We cut Max's workdays down from 6:00am – 9:00pm to 7:00am – 6:00pm. Still long days by any regular standard, but a huge improvement for him and much more typical in the world of healthy CEOs.

Max and I met a few times to help him get the hang of his new schedule, and I also met with his management team and attended an operations meeting to introduce the concepts of time zones throughout the organization. Max would have a much easier time getting buy-in from his staff around planning when they would meet on certain subjects instead of just popping in whenever they liked if they, too, were planning their own time. Max was unsure about it at first – he didn't like the idea of sounding like he was complaining about being overworked. But we rolled it out as a company wellness initiative and his team was hugely enthusiastic – this, frankly, is exactly that they had been waiting for. Many were working beyond their own capacity, as well, trying to keep up with Max as he tried to be there for them, and most breathed a sigh of relief as we began to shift the culture toward focus, engagement and peak performance instead of blood, sweat and tears.

Soon Max began to feel like he could breathe again, just a little. He told me his wife reported she could see a difference in that he was starting to look less tired, which was great to hear. I reminded him that I had said from the outset it would take three to six months to really integrate these changes and see full benefits, and a year or more beyond that of continuous mindfulness to be able to say "no turning back," yet I too was very excited at how well things were going.

As big as these scheduling changes were, they were the means, not the end. Our goal had been to give Max more time and energy for the things he cared about that were beyond simply getting his job done and getting enough sleep, to lay a foundation that would make more abundant goals possible. Business, professionalism, doing a good job, providing service – all these mattered to Max, but, in terms of an entire life, they added up to only one important element out of many highly valued areas. To find the balance he described himself as seeking, he would have to prioritize and contextualize the things he cared about. If you thought it was hard to get him on a schedule at work…

I alluded earlier to some of Max's core values. When you see the list of scheduled activities stemming from each value for just one week, the problem becomes obvious. Plus signs (+) indicate commuting times and/or probable activity overruns which have not otherwise been accounted for.

Education & Professional Development: Board of Trade (3 hours+); Servant Leadership Course (3.5 hours for class, 3 hours for reading and homework+); Bookstore/Other Reading (4 hours+)

Spirituality: Sunday Gathering (2-3 hours); Tuesday Abundance Class (3 hours+)

Community Engagement: Presentation by Doctors Without Borders (3 hours+); Volunteering with Junior Achievement (2 hours+); Fundraising for Chamber Music Festival (4 hours+)

Family & Friends: Time with wife and children (10 hours); Dinner with A (3 hours); Lunch with B (1.5 hours); Phone Calls with C, D & E (2 hours); Email (2 hours)

Health and Fitness: Run Club that he wanted to join as part of his plan with his doctor to lower his cardio-vascular health risks (5 hours+); Weekly Weight Training Boot Camp (1.5 hours+)

Solace/Quiet Time: Gulf Island Overnight Retreat (32 hours+)

Though most of us never stop to count them, there are 168 hours in a week. (Less than you thought, I bet, huh?) Assuming 49 hours each week for sleep at 7 hours per night, and 50 hours per week for work, plus 10.5 hours for getting ready and having breakfast each morning and having lunch each afternoon at 1.5 hours per day, we've got $168 - 109.5 = 58.50$ hours remaining available for life that is neither sleep, self care nor work. The activities listed above add up to 85.5 hours on their own!

And, though every hour was already over-subscribed, this schedule didn't allow for commuting anywhere, or for shopping or preparing meals, doing housekeeping or errands, let alone having anything unexpected happen. In short, this lifestyle was incompatible with the realities of standard life maintenance. Even if everything went exactly as according to plan, Max was already almost 30 hours behind schedule at the start of this very typical week. I suspect he knew even as he booked it he would not actually take his retreat – cancelling that which might restore him had become a habit, as had truncating time with many important people in all facets of his life. With so little rest, self care and inspiration, Max was dangerously depleting himself. The right mix of activities, even stressors, is generative, energizing. But Max wasn't giving himself any chance to experience energy's natural flow. No wonder he was exhausted – this kind of stress and guilt would eat away at anyone, but especially someone trying so hard to be dependable.

It was *because* he felt so honour-bound to be connected that cutting activities was extremely challenging for Max. His model had been one of striving every day to do everything on his list and more or less letting fate make cuts for him when time simply ran out. And, frankly, I found it challenging at times to refute the advisability of such sound, upright choices. After all, there is no mindless television-watching or aimless retail therapy in his schedule. Max's wish-list of activities is filled with things that are healthy for him and good for society, too. What could be bad about that? Every time I thought I had found something to cut, he'd have a compelling rebuttal: "Doctors Without Borders is an excellent organization – I've always wanted to learn more about their work and now is my chance"; "That's a travelling exhibit, so if I don't see it this week, I'll never see it"; "That friend has been having a really rough time and he's been loyal; I owe it to him to show up."

Max's wants were also powerfully virtuous *shoulds* – powerful enough to obligate him right into a near-constant state of overwhelm. No doubt some of you can see yourselves in this story: your Doctors Without Borders lecture might be a play or concert or networking event; your art exhibit a baby shower or trade show; your friend in need a busy spouse or an active child, but the syndrome is the same. How do we choose between equally valued, equally attractive options and make them fit inside the rigid structure of a 24-hour day? How do we devote enough energy to the activities of life to enjoy and benefit from them and have enough energy left over for the not-so-simple living of life?

I invited Max to start thinking of his life in phases, stages, cycles... whatever ease-ful, flow-y, abundant metaphor would resonate for him. The sense of 'must do it all TODAY' is what creates all the pushing and panicking, not the draw to the activities themselves. When my clients are multi-talented, multi-dimensional, multi-joyful people drawn to multi-faceted lives (and I'm sure you must be getting by now that this is the majority of the time), I encourage them to consider a series of one, three or even five year life cycles which will allow the tangible expression of his heartfelt passions to gently move into different levels of priority so that all may be accommodated over a life well-lived.

Max's 'metaphor'? "Oh, right, five year plans. Like Mao and Stalin. I get it." Well, not exactly where I was going, but at least he'd found a frame of reference, and if he wasn't bothered by the associations, I wasn't going to worry about it. Stalin! Okay, let's roll! We determined that, given his age, the stage of his family's development, and the stage of his business's development, it made sense to focus more on family and business now, with community moving up in prominence as his children and his employees needed him less. I had some concerns that this would create some anxiety for Max at first; I anticipated him feeling that we were taking some of his passions away. I was surprised – pleasantly so, of course, when he got on board so quickly. Once he understood that everything he cared about would have a place, nothing would be left out, just apportioned differently, he relaxed and began to enjoy himself.

For two years Max kept his energy high, living in integrity with a schedule in which he was home for dinner five nights per week, spent dedicated time with his children many evenings and every weekend, and protected leadership and reflective time from meeting mania and urgency overwhelm, all the while improving his health, creating a wellness culture at the office and – not insignificantly – growing revenues beyond projections as well. (In case you were wondering, values-driven business is good ROI…) Then one day Max called me again to say we had to go back to work.

"Alanna, I know this stuff works so I'm ready to do what you tell me," said Max, "but we need to do it on different targets now, sooner than we planned. I feel like I'm still missing some things with my kids that I want to be there for – they're in those teenager years when they barely want to see me, but, when they do want me, it can't wait to be scheduled, I have to be there, ready. I want more flexibility. And the company is stable enough now that I'm thinking I might be ready to start handing off the day-to-day operations. Other things are calling, so I'm calling you."

Exciting news! I believe plans are great tools if they are held lightly, encouraged to be fluid and allowed to grow – even to die and be reborn. Making a plan and then following it line-by-line, even if it includes flextime or open space, is still a way of dying a little inside. Max had found his spark of life and he wasn't letting it go: that, more than anything else, is what he was telling me on this day. So we went to work figuring out (a) what was calling and what it was saying and (b) what systems he would need in place to answer the call.

As we explored together over a few hours where he was experiencing the greatest joy and flow, and conversely where he was feeling more flat, less inspired, it appeared that the stability in the business wasn't attractive to him. He had loved the start-up and the rapid growth years, this actually his third start-up in a leadership role. Now that they had perfected everything, a big part of what made it juicy for him was gone. And what was exciting? Two things: a young entrepreneur's program where he had been volunteering one half-day a month (all start-up all the time – just his passion!) and a program for teens through the spiritual centre he attended. He wanted to work in his business no more than about ten hours per week and be able to be with his own kids and other young people at this stage of his life. These passions had long been central to five year plans two and three: we were just moving them up.

So we worked together for about four months on a plan to transfer operational responsibility to one of Max's senior team leads, Patrick, and to create the schedule he wanted. We focused on creating institutional memory, documenting systems, codifying company values and culture, and capacity-building from top down, bottom up and sideways with leadership

> I believe plans are great tools if they are held lightly, encouraged to be fluid and allowed to grow – even to die and be reborn. Making a plan and then following it line-by-line, even if it includes flextime or open space, is still a way of dying a little inside.

development, mentorship, cross-training and peer coaching programs designed and ready for implementation the following year. (I should be clear that while my strategic involvement increased to eight to ten hours per week during this time, Max's team took this and ran with it and the credit is theirs.)

Just as we were starting to look at what sort of vision Max had for his community contributions, he asked to see me on short notice – and he sounded upset. "Patrick is quitting," came the shocking news as Max was barely in the door. "He says he is not getting the support he needs from some of the staff who still turn to me; he says he doesn't believe I will ever stop having the authority of the Founder; he says that he doesn't want it like this. There goes my retirement."

"Okay, Max," I replied, "I'm going to ask you to sit down, breathe, forget you're a male CEO for a moment and tell this to me like you are one of your teenage daughters, okay? Tell it like a girl – all the context, chronological order, every detail: 'I was wearing and he was wearing and I said and then he said,' okay? We'll get through this but I need to have as complete a picture as I can." This served to get Max to laugh for a second, changing the energy just enough for us both to feel more open, and got him breaking it all down.

The crux of it seemed to me to be a lot of bereavement and acting out behaviours stemming from that grief. "How can Patrick be grieving when I haven't left yet and he's getting a promotion and a whole bunch more money?" Max asked incredulously.

"Well, feelings don't have to be logical," I responded, "but in this case they kind of are. Your employees love you and you them; however excited you might be about this future, you are all also fighting it because of the inevitable loss of daily closeness. My sense is you probably are grabbing the reins a little tighter on these last days and other employees are reaching out to you for one last touch and Patrick is feeling guilty because he is personally benefiting from what everyone – including him and including you – see as a short term loss to your community."

I asked Max for permission to speak to Patrick to see if we could dial down the acting out by exploring the feelings more directly. I spent three hours with Patrick the following day – pulled him out of his office to walk Vancouver's beautiful 10km seawall with me – and eventually got to all the mixed feelings he'd been having. He was mad at Max for leaving him, mad at himself for not taking advantage of the opportunity, mad at people for not listening to him, mad at having to feel bad about what should be a great opportunity. And eventually he also admitted that he didn't want to quit – he couldn't even believe that he had said it and he really wanted to take it back.

"Okay, well that part's done," I said. "Max wasn't going to accept a resignation, anyway, and you know it – that's why it was safe to quit." Patrick smiled as I continued: "Here's my thing, and you can tell me how this sits with you. My belief has long been that we are rarely really *angry*. Anger is a socially acceptable, not-very-vulnerable emotion that we default to when there are less validated, less safe emotions we feel we can't express. What do you think?"

"I guess that could be true," came Patrick's reply, and we were quickly able to get to the heart of the fear and sadness that he and all the employees were feeling at this time. I went back to Max and asked him to consider bringing a grief counsellor in to work with his team. He balked at first, as had become our pattern: I suggest; he protests; I persist; he acquiesces; and together we both laugh.

In that process (which would take another book to explain, someone else's, so apologies for leaving you hanging on that part), it became clear to everyone that what needed to happen was for Patrick to buy the company from Max outright and take it over fully – clear roles, clean break. A couple of investors from among the management team and a couple of good lawyers and a deal was struck for a buy-out over five years, with Max as an external consultant during that time and receiving residual payments, to himself and/or his heirs, as long as the company remained in business.

The plan was good and the work was great: *and* the work/life intention was better served by being open to what showed up. Fast Tracks show us the truth of the age-old aphorism: "All the world will step aside to let you pass if you only know where you are going."

Chapter 4

Letters After Your Name:

Credentialing and Confidence

There are many more ways to get an education and to advance up professional ranks than either heading off to university at 18 and staying there until you are fully cooked or re-mortgaging your home at midlife to go back to school full time and pick up the books you left behind in your salad days. I'm a big fan of education and a bigger fan of the way it is becoming more accessible at all stages of life. And I often attract clients who are looking for a way to customize their credentialing to fit their lives even more than it does in even the most evolved designs as advertised. Even programs built with three or four stretchy sizes do not fit *all*, and my preference is to help working people work and learn in an integrated way.

Bethany, the client whose story I'll relate here, is emblematic of people with whom I typically work in a number of ways: in how she became a client; in aspects of her experience of gender, age, and workplace dynamic; in the creative approaches we took to making drivers out of perceived barriers; in the validation and empowerment well beyond professional development she experienced in securing new letters after her name; and in the satisfaction which happily resulted for her. (Yeah, I know, I gave away the ending: but you never really thought I was going to tell tragic stories here, right? This book is a celebration of love, end to end!)

Many of my clients come to me in a moment of urgency with a very specific objective for why we are doing the work:

> "My kids are almost university age and I can't pay their tuition at the rate I'm going. I need to earn more in these next 3-5 crucial years so I can give them the future we all want."

> "My boss is a micro-managing, sarcastic, sniping, multiple-personality Neanderthal and I can't work there one week longer! Get me out!"

> "I am an accountant. Numbers and spreadsheets every day, all day. But suddenly, after ten years of reasonable success and what I thought was enjoyment at my career, I can't get myself to care about it in the slightest anymore. Nothing makes sense. I need you to help me get back to normal."

Or, as in Bethany's case:

> "My whole industry is completely sexist and no one takes me seriously. I want to administer a 360 degree evaluation of the whole organization that will show how blocked women are in the company and then I want you to help me demand the promotion I have deserved for over four years."

In these times, we begin with intensity, emotional honesty, clarity, desire... and almost always also pain, fear, anger, emotional blocking, resistance and lack of perspective. Many great truths are paradoxes: we often get to a place of knowing ourselves and accessing our power through the very experience of first telling ourselves a story in which we are cast as a victim – and then revising the narrative when we realize we don't like how it reads. Often my clients and I embark on the work as ordered up only to find very different reasons, a quite unique purpose, just beneath the surface of the exploration – and arrive at wonderful destinations well off the course initially proposed. I could feel somehow that this would be the case for Bethany, even as I didn't know what either the destination or the course would be.

I don't force people to do work they don't want to do. I do insist on some values clarification and needs assessment before we launch into any discreet project, but then we see what happens. And what almost invariably happens is that somewhere along the line, the client says, "Man, I'm having a bad day. There's a lot of stuff coming up for me that I didn't expect." And I know today is the day they'll look back on as a very good day. One of the best days. The day we got to do the real stuff. The day they started coming back to life. And so it begins.

For Bethany, the stuff she didn't expect took the form of the data results gathered in the 360 evaluation on which she had contracted me to consult (for those of you who don't speak human resources or organizational development jargon, a 360 is a collection of quantitative and qualitative feedback, collated and cross-referenced, about people, performance, policies, systems, cultures, etc., from as many members of an organizational team as possible, the "360 degrees" connoting input from all angles). It turned out that almost none of the other mid- to senior-level women in the organization felt there was any significant discrimination on the basis of gender – or on any other basis for that matter. In response to both quantitative and qualitative questions, around 26 of 30 women project managers, senior associates and partners surveyed in the regional office of Bethany's large consulting engineering firm said, in sum, that they felt the company was quite progressive and that promotions were given out on the basis of merit.

The consistency in the responses only made Bethany more angry as she insisted that in her rarified world of highly specialized engineering, the professors were male, the partners were male and the ideologies were male, and she demanded that I re-do the survey. I explained that the data was collected in as blind a way as possible, with people able to complete the surveys on their own time, from any computer, with IP addresses obscured by encryption and no need to self-identify except with checkboxes for demographic information and, with so many respondents, there would be no way to identify any one person by her demographic information. Thus, one had to ask, on what basis would anyone need to misrepresent her views?

I understood then as I do now how masculinist many cultures in the hard sciences and applied sciences can be: I've worked with hundreds of clients in those fields; indeed, well before I entered coaching and consulting, one of my first professional jobs was to teach literature and rhetoric to a class made up almost entirely of engineering students. (Not my finest hour at first, my 22 year-old knees shaking beneath the very grown-up suits in which I tried desperately to hide, but I won them over and it was a great experience learning how to do that.) I could also accept that one or two respondents might not feel safe with the confidentiality of the process, leading them to skew some of their answers. But to believe that so many professional women, all of them technically savvy enough to know how the blind data collection process worked, would be too scared to say they had experienced any discrimination? It just didn't add up for me, so I couldn't recommend repeating the process with a different assessment tool.

To say Bethany was not warm to my response at first would be a gross understatement. I believe words were used to the effect that I was being paid to do what I was told. After I explained that I have never in my life accepted money on those terms and I wouldn't be starting that day, I asked Bethany if perhaps she thought *she* was being paid to do what she was told, and whether that might be an area we could explore together. She fumed for quite awhile longer but, eventually – after realizing she had begun shouting and tearing up, and then hearing herself saying, "This place is a cesspool of sexism and I can't believe someone like you can't see it!" – she did come around to the idea that there might be some exploration for her to do and working with me was as good a place as any to start.

As I was recently reminded by a sage and compassionate friend when I was myself creating drama in reaction to some new self awareness, when we feel like we are losing our minds, losing our selves, losing our identities, chances are what we're really losing is our *perspective*. Reclaiming it usually means taking more than a few steps back to look at a much bigger picture than we first set out to see.

My first question to Bethany at this point was why she was working at this firm. "What the hell else am I going to do with an engineering degree?" came her angrily reflexive response which didn't strike me as very real. I told her I thought she was an extremely talented and capable woman and she knew as well as I did that with her education and life skills, there were a lot of other things she could have done if she wanted to. Besides which, I added, we had begin our journey together trying to her get a promotion: smart people don't usually work harder to get deeper into organizations they hate. So what's up?

We went back and forth for about twenty minutes with Bethany saying that at her stage of life (just 42, for goodness sake – hardly a 'stage' except for growing into herself, I'd argue!), she had to make the best of a bad situation, and me repeatedly saying some version of "Hell, no, you don't! No one does!" and offering to start work on getting her out of there immediately if it was so bad.

Then Bethany finally said, "Alright – there are some advantages I tend to forget about when I get angry. Consulting work lets me go from project to project, concept to completion, really get deeply into intense work for periods of a few months, then back off and catch my breath, work on a few proposals, and then launch into another big project. The rhythm of it suits my temperament."

"Okay, good. There's got to be more to it than that, though," I said. "You sounded pretty miserable not very long ago, so you're going to have to convince me why you would even consider staying, why I shouldn't call all your friends to have an intervention right now and yank you out of there."

Bethany had worked up so much anger that was working against her, I thought it was time for some to work in her favour: arguing *against* me and *for* her chosen profession might help her find what she loved about it again, doing the double duty of burning off some of that pent up energy so we'd have more space for her to soften, as well. And if she couldn't win the debate to her own satisfaction, then we'd know for sure it was time for her to move on. It was a gamble, but it paid off.

We spent another half hour talking about some of her more interesting projects, crazy all-nighters putting RFPs together, the giggles she and her teammates get over pizza in small town motel rooms as they collate data gathered on remote location and brainstorm solutions to sticky situations, and the satisfaction of knowing that something is built soundly, safely and

> I had goose bumps, too. Bethany had found the poetry of her work experience again. It was starting to sound like love to me...

smoothly as a result of her work. The more I said I didn't know if she really wanted to be an engineer, if she really cared enough about those people to invest another fifteen years of her life, or really saw herself with any kind of future happiness in a stuffy consulting firm, the more confidently she came back with the goodness of it all.

"It's hard to explain to someone who doesn't do this work. Grids and gradients, CAD drawings and calculations don't sound very creative or inspiring, I know. And rooms full of people wearing khaki pants and approach shoes to the office, pocket protectors on half the guys," she laughed, "I get it that it doesn't look very sexy. But there is something amazing about what we do."

She paused for a moment, taking a time out to actually *be* amazed again, then continued.

"We make something out of nothing. We solve impossible problems in very creative ways. We see things other people don't even imagine and then actually figure out how to build them. We take things apart, see how they are made, then build something even better, more innovative. And it's very team-oriented, sharing that vision, pulling together to make things happen. I knew I wanted to be an engineer or an architect because it's where art and science meet. That's the thing about *Applied* Science, right: it's all that great theory, all the universal laws and what makes everything tick, and then we actually make it useful to people. Even with all the unenlightened communication, sometimes messy politics, late nights and bad food, when I think about that, I still get goose bumps."

I had goose bumps, too. Bethany had found the poetry of her work experience again. It was starting to sound like love to me...

"So what would we have to do," I asked, "to change your career to one where you feel about it all the time the way you are feeling right now?"

"If I knew that, I'd have done it already," she grumbled.

"Well, there is knowing and then there is *knowing*," I replied. "There is the easily accessible, out front daily knowing of surface-y things and perhaps a few life lessons we have well integrated and therefore deepened, but still outside-in. And then there is the knowing of the soul, the inner sense of who we are and what matters to us that we are born with, that is inside-out, but that we let get buried under the burdens of life sometimes. Go back to the woman who loves holding the vision with her team. In fact, close your eyes for a moment and let's see if you can call it up now."

I asked Bethany to see herself in the northern mill town motel room she had talked about a few minutes before, pizza boxes on the bed, empty Corona bottles scattered around, a circle of colleagues sitting cross-legged on a grungy carpet, CAD printouts strewn around and a couple of laptops open on chair seats and balanced on kneecaps... and Bethany in the heart of it, telling a story about the day that was making everyone laugh. As she relaxed into that space, I invited her to recall some of the conversation, see how people were responding to her, and feel her feelings in that moment.

After a nice long pause to let her take that in, I asked her what she had seen and felt. Bethany realized that she felt strongest in groups of peers and subordinates – very different from the stuckness and resentment she often felt around those above her in the hierarchy. When she had what she called "standing" – some authority, power...

"Or when you are standing in your power?" I offered, and she smiled, saying okay, yes, that might be one way to look at it. When she was in touch with that standing, it was easy to be open, to experience herself as excited and connected, to be part of the team.

"What felt connected – in the motel room, specifically?" I asked.

"They see me," came Bethany's reply – quickly, with some surprise, yet also a solid tenor to her voice.

"Or you let yourself be seen," I countered.

"Yeah," said Bethany. "It's sort of like… for me to remember to laugh, I need to feel taken seriously, be respected."

"So the promotion is about recognition, validation?" I checked in, and she nodded yes.

"What about salary, challenge, maybe decision-making or budgetary authority?"

"All those things are good and I'll take them for sure," Bethany said, "but it's really about being seen. I feel like it's time I was acknowledged for what I can do."

"Okay," I said. "But that's going to have to start with you, and I think you know that. If you're game to take a long and appreciative look at yourself, I know I am, and I think between the two of us we can make that promotion happen."

Sexual discrimination no longer the central issue, we did still need to better see what tended to help or hinder a promotion track in her company, thus Bethany and I began doing some analysis of the differences between her career path, her unique experience of her profession and her framing of that experience, and the career paths and skill sets of some of the women who had risen through the ranks of her large firm more quickly than she had. This was not an easy thing for Bethany to do: though she had uncovered a new sense of herself, she also had many years of habitual thinking to cope with and she oscillated back and forth on her relative openness to the idea that other women were, in fact, advancing.

In deference to Bethany's training in scientific inquiry, we tried to focus primarily on factual information at this stage. I asked her to bring me the company organizational chart and I went through it, identifying women's names, cross-referencing them to corporate bios where possible and otherwise asking Bethany what she knew or could find out about these people. This method would not account for every variable – it could not, for example, say for sure who might have better leveraged relationships or personal ties to improve their individual chances for advancement – but it could reveal certain commonalities worth considering.

We narrowed our search to a pool of a dozen women who Bethany agreed she respected; who were plus or minus ten years of Bethany's age to be at a relatively similar stage of career; and who, irrespective of division or job title, had positioned themselves for what would generally be regarded as significantly more responsibility or compensation than Bethany had to this point (these last criteria as relatively objective measures of recognition and power in the organization). Then we looked for patterns.

Bethany noticed that, to her recollection, several of them had worked at one time or another for one of two partners in the organization who were widely known for their ability to develop talent – something which, as an outsider, I would not have caught or initially perceived as significant. "Wow," she commented each time one of these two names came up, "That was seven years ago, I'd forgotten all about it, but she worked for him, too. This can't be a coincidence." No, I didn't think it was a coincidence, either. If nine of twelve senior women in the organization had the same kind of mentorship, whether they proactively chose their mentors (as I would bet many of them did) or they just got lucky (as Bethany at first believed), my view is those statistics are worth following up.

The first thing that I noticed is that all of them had some education outside of engineering. "That can't be right," Bethany argued. But their bios didn't lie: Four had MBAs; two had Bachelor's degrees in Commerce or Arts; two had advanced certification in Project Management; one had an undergrad degree in Accounting; another had done work in ISO quality systems; one was a green belt in Six Sigma; and one had come in via a Liberal Arts and Communications program. A pretty accomplished group, I'd say, and definitely suggesting the firm had a strong bias toward broad skill sets in its senior engineers, not a bias against women. "Oh," came Bethany's response. (Making her speechless had to be a good thing...)

The rest of our admittedly unempirical study was equally instructive for its *lack* of patterns: some of the women had started into engineering right out of high school; others not until their early thirties. Some were single, no kids; others partnered and juggling children or aging parents. Some were working in the specialized field for which they had studied; others had jumped specialties at least once or even twice over the course of their career. Some were extremely well-liked at all levels of the organization; others had ruffled a lot of feathers along the way and had a few key allies but no chance of winning a popularity contest.

So there it was: mentorship and education. We knew exactly what Bethany needed to do if she wanted to advance. I was tickled pink. Bethany was nearly apoplectic.

First, we were of course challenging nearly every significant belief she had held about her discipline, her company and herself. Engineering wasn't entirely sexist? Education and credentials not only mattered for advancement, but her firm seemed – gulp – progressively interested in learning outside the narrow bounds of science? Relationships counted more than revenue generation? Power was found inside herself?

"I guess I didn't get that memo," Bethany laughed nervously as we talked this through, her mind obviously reeling but her spirit, I was glad to see, game to step up to the challenge. And it was about as challenging as any confrontation of beliefs can get. Work is a place of self-definition and in accepting just one new perspective on her workplace and her self in that workplace, Bethany found dozens of other new perspectives pressing to be acknowledged.

Think about it: if Bethany could have had a promotion by making some different choices a few years ago, then she was feeling like everything she thought and knew was being called into question. That wasn't true, of course. Except where it was.

That's the paradox of this kind of learning: it's not a discreet, contained, one lesson deal. It has implications, consequences. Usually very good ones, eventually, as we process and assimilate. But first our assumptions, perceptions and core beliefs are rocked way off balance, shaking up everything we think we know is true before settling again to find their centre.

Second, Bethany had signed up for a 360 evaluation which she expected would show that she had been owed a promotion for a very long time and thus she would get one – from that process alone. Now we were talking about grad school, career management, mentorship... no blame, no entitlement, and the very real prospect of a lot of work. She wasn't sure she wanted to do it. In fact, I'd have to say she was pretty sure she didn't want to: she cancelled her next appointment and didn't call me for over a month. I sent a nudge email or two in that time to let her know I was still there, but had to give her the space she was asking for.

> Think about it: if Bethany could have had a promotion by making some different choices a few years ago, then she was feeling like everything she thought and knew was being called into question. That wasn't true, of course. Except where it was.

When she did call me again, she was ready to jump in with... well, about three toes. I'm a fan of immersion but I can do the inch-by-inch easing thing if that's what a client really feels is needed (or just the only way they will play along). I know at a certain point they all plug their nose and just do it, anyway, so whatever it takes to get there, I'm in for the ride. Bethany agreed that we would look at training program options and that I could give her a maximum of three hours of homework every two weeks: she was busy and did not have a lot of time to fool around. Though that sounded like an oxymoron to me, I went with it for the moment. Two weeks to look at project management programs. Two weeks to research Master's programs in engineering. Two weeks of MBA programs. Whoa, there are a lot of them! Two more weeks of MBA programs. Two weeks to look at — wait, what were we looking at again, she asked? My point exactly.

"Bethany," I said, "Your biggest argument against going back to school and seeking mentorship is how long it would take, that you are 42 and will still be in university at the same time as your kids are in university, and you'll be 'ooold' before you see any benefits. How are we helping this by taking so long to do it that we can't even remember what we were talking about last time? It's February now. I know for a fact that most university and college applications need to be in within the next six weeks for you to be considered for September. You're in charge and I'll back whatever decision you make, but my two cents is we should make this happen now. If you are accepted, you can decide to defer your enrolment for as much as two years in some cases; if you don't apply, you have no options."

I won't pretend there weren't grumblings, but because we started the conversation from Bethany's own awareness of her dissociation on the long and winding road, she agreed to get on the education highway with me – at least for a little while.

After comparing a number of programs offering all on-site classes, hybrids of evenings, weekends and teleconferences, and those based on an entirely distance education model, Bethany chose to apply to two of the hybrid MBA programs. She chose an MBA over other options because it had the most 'teeth' as we called it – diverse learning and challenge to get her juices going, prestige and credibility, a chance to be at the centre of the action in terms of decision-making and money, and even transferability out of engineering if she someday felt she wanted something different after all. Both programs offered lots of flexibility in terms of time and learning styles but would also allow her to build relationships and get important emotional and social support on this journey.

Now came time for putting together the application package: she needed an exhaustive CV, a biographical resume which charted her career journey by milestones and achievements, a statement of interest and intention, and four reference letters, two of which had to come from within her firm. I thought that last part was a very good thing because I wanted to add to our To Do List a proposal for the firm to sponsor or at least subsidize her education, which would mean creating a rationale for why it was as advantageous to them as it was to her.

Bethany did great with the CV and resume – every *i* dotted and *t* crossed on time for my edits as promised, but struggled with the references. Work that you can hand off to someone else is usually the easiest thing to do, so I was a little surprised and asked what was up. "I gave them the application materials over a week ago and no one has gotten back to me. Five people to get four references and no response," said Bethany, obviously distressed. I was relieved: she had done her part, so it wasn't resistance. Overworked and not-overly-writerly engineers we could deal with. "That's great news," I replied.

Bethany looked at me puzzled but I stood by my words: when something that we know can and should be easy *isn't*, I think it's always a sign that we could be doing it another way and enjoy a better result. Sometimes that means doing something else entirely because we're on the wrong track and our higher self knows it. In this case, my gut said we could take more control of the process, help Bethany step more into her own recognition and empowerment of herself.

We reviewed the MBA application criteria again and isolated different aspects of her performance to highlight to match groupings they were looking for. I then gave Bethany the assignment of pulling together all of the specific examples and achievements from her career which would substantiate her high performance in even more detail than her resume, and to add to it a list of her strengths and qualities that she would want her referees to recognize and vouch for. This was a great opportunity to turn what had been a barrier into a driver, to make the delay work for us and make the outcome even better than we first imagined.

Once Bethany pulled her self assessment together, and really owned her heroic career success stories, she felt palpably more confident about her application. Then it was my turn. I took her content and used it to write the recommendation letters she would need, carefully using a different voice, varied sentence structure and unique turns of phrase for each. A focus on leadership ability in one, business acumen in another, technical project skills in a third, etc. – the very 360 degree evaluation she had started out wanting, just a much more helpful and empowering version of it, if I do say so myself. She rocked on paper! Every bit as much as in life.

Bethany waited a few more days then approached each potential referee with a steaming latte in one hand and the recommendation she needed on letterhead in the other and said "I know you're busy so I thought it might help if I gave you a head start. Feel free to change anything to make it sound more like you, of course..."

Every one of them signed it on the spot! Naturally Bethany received early acceptance to both MBA programs...

Getting in is one thing. Getting through is another, as anyone who has ever juggled full time work with full time family and part time graduate school will tell you – if they can stop long enough to talk to you, that is. Bethany worried about upgrading her laptop and buying a nice leather knapsack; I focused on getting buy-in from the folks she'd need to mentor her. My plan went like this: put together a draft funding proposal asking for her tuition and for a four-day reduced workweek during the last six weeks of each semester when the workload would get tight; make a case for the firm's return-on-investment which included specifics about future projects currently under bid on which she could use her new skills and increase her charge-out rate; take the draft proposal to the two known mentors of leading women in the firm for feedback and ask them to help take it up the food chain, thereby both sparking their interest in her and boosting her chances of getting her proposal accepted. Any time you can get one piece of work to do two (or three or four) things for you, take it!

It took a couple of stabs to get the proposal to where it needed to be – mostly because the mentors took a real interest and offered some excellent ideas we needed to incorporate – but by the time she sat her first exam, Bethany had a commitment from the firm to reimburse all of her costs at the end of each semester (tuition, books, even long distance telephone and parking fees), and to grant her four day workweeks going forward from her second term with no change to her salary. That's four days *every* week she was in school – not just the six weeks per term we asked for. (That nice plug came from her new mentor... if this were email, there'd be a blinking happy face right here _____.)

At the end of that all-important first term, Bethany came to see me for a follow-up session and shed a few tears as she grappled with her demanding study schedule; hundreds of new words and foreign concepts; and her husband and kids complaining that she hardly made dinner anymore (not that they had especially liked her cooking before, apparently, but big changes cause anxiety to manifest in all kinds of ways, including adolescents deciding they now miss the broccoli they used to refuse to eat). Everything was getting harder at once! Yes, that's how it usually goes. Growth is multi-directional, multi-dimensional.

We worked on a script for how she could explain her need to stretch out, prove herself and be recognized to her family (the advantage of her kids being adolescent is that they had these same desires in common with their mom in a big way right now). We put together a time map which put her schedule into time zones for different kinds of activities, adding much-needed perspective and making decisions easier.

We also worked through the major tenets of Jim Loehr's *The Power of Full Engagement*, a four-part program for achieving peak performance in spiritual, emotional, mental and physical dimensions which I became certified to deliver in Canada. I love the focus on spirituality as a driver and physicality as a foundation, with intellect and heart included as well for holistic balance. Fortunately, Bethany related very well to the structure the program gave her at a time of great pressure and stress. Bethany kept a 15 minute tune-up coaching call with me every week just to remind her why she was doing what she was doing and what she loved about it on the days she would inevitably forget.

On another day a few months later, Bethany was again in tears in my office: this time because she had received the first *A+* grade of her academic career.

And her story has a great addendum, too. In a search for recognition and validation, "Letters After Your Name" can be a big flop unless you consciously choose to make them meaningful. As most of us learn at some point in the first few years after university, no one really cares what your GPA was once you graduate. And, FYI, no one comes to offer you a raise and a better life just because you have new credentials. You create your success; you don't wait for it. Once Bethany fully understood that – indeed, that recognition, you'll recall, was prerequisite to her even starting an MBA, let along finishing one – a whole lot more things than just her career opened up for her. By the time she got the degree, the promotion and the raise, things had shifted so far those goals were barely relevant. She was grateful for them, of course – but, having found recognition within herself, she also wound up caring much less about them in the end than the other, more joyful, features she added to her life in a completely unexpected-serendipitous-yet-intentional way.

By the end of her second semester, several 'As' to her credit and the equanimity to not mind the *B* in the course she didn't fall in love with, Bethany took the fear-busting spirit of adventure and self-love that came to life inside her and began taking kayaking lessons, something that had always scared her before and shut her out of a great deal of fun as her husband and two children went out on all-day water adventures she used to miss. She also decided to put an end to the lie she had been telling herself that, as a mother and a busy professional and now also a student, she could not travel like she used to when she was young. Where she once had taken big, juicy trips involving planes, trains and automobiles to quite literally the four corners of the earth, in recent years she had chosen visiting relatives, taking her kids to theme parks and jet-ski-umbrella-drink beaches. Nothing wrong with either of those (I'll personally take the latter any time I can get it), but it wasn't the kind of getaway that spoke to Bethany's heart.

Once she stopped making excuses about 'being a girl' and 'needing to do what she was told' at work, she was free to stop making them anywhere she chose, and she celebrated by spending two weeks on an eco-tour in Costa Rica – kayaking, of course! – and showing her kids that their mom still had a lot of game in her.

Chapter 5

Making Lemonade:

(...When Your Job Is a Lemon But Leaving Isn't an Option)

When life gives you lemons, it is said, you're supposed to make lemonade. When life knocks you on your ass, *bounce*! I subscribe to those beliefs in the broad sense of wanting to encourage forward movement, being creative. I challenge the assumption, however, that we must sit passively to see what flavour of citrus we are 'given' in this life, and say let's start creating right out of thin air!

The 'lemons' I most often see in my clients' lives take the form of physical and emotional health problems caused or exacerbated by a disconnect between their values and their work. It doesn't have to be as bad as the 'toxic workplaces' we read about: any substantial and unabated gap between you and what you really want can feel toxic in your experience of it. Lowered energy and blue mood; headaches and back pain at the slightest provocation; colds and allergies that never go away – these kinds of life-dragging symptoms are your higher self's way of telling you that you might well be in the wrong place. Problem is, we often don't listen for a long, bleak, sad, tired, immune depleted, barely-recognize-ourselves time.

Asked to recall times when they felt "switched on," "psyched up," "on top of things," many people find themselves unable to come up with examples. Alternatingly overwhelmed by emotion and disconnected from feeling, they reschedule appointments, feign pet emergencies and traffic jams, and create all sorts of other dramas for discussion to avoid the subject. Or, if they are like my client, Skye, they go for kicking and screaming and attacking the coach instead. (We're both fine, as you'll see from Skye's story below…)

Skye was so far down the energy black hole that she couldn't even remember anything that she liked to do. In fact, she was so far gone that she was frankly pissed off that I would even suggest she could have something so radical as "hobbies" or "interests."

"Those days are over for me," Skye said. "I just need a better job and I'll be fine." Makes you feel kind of warm and fuzzy, doesn't it? I certainly felt motivated to do my level best. I'm being ironic, of course, but that part's actually true. Because while Skye was often cranky and pretty much always sullen in those early days, I could also see that she was a really bright woman. And I knew that she was highly valued by the friend who had referred her to me, which meant she could connect with people. I saw hope even when it was hiding – and hiding very well.

Skye had a gorgeous vintage briefcase – supple, thick, rich leather, the kind you can't get anymore because they split leather into two and three sheets and layer it up with coating to get more out of each calfskin (I spent one abominable Christmas season in my undergrad years working in a leather goods store – so not my calling! – but my brain has a way of retaining the darnedest information and today I would make it useful…). When I told her how gorgeous her briefcase was and asked where she got it, I was treated to a full 90 seconds where she had an actual personality. Skye's eyes verily sparkled just long enough for this exchange: "Madrid. An open air market in Madrid."

"I bet there's a story there…" I offered.

And she replied, "Yeah, I haggled," and started to laugh before catching herself (she had decided she could no longer be a woman who laughs, after all, and she was blowing her own cover). She recovered her gloom and hastily closed down our dialogue with "But my days of exotic trips are over. I just need a job that pays the bills and doesn't make me want to throw up every afternoon. Can you help me or not?"

Ah, that warmed the cockles of my heart. I like demanding clients – it means there's passion there. And I'll take open hostility over covert resistance any day; a little hot anger has much more potential than listlessness and apathy. She was working hard not to admit it to anyone, but Skye still cared. And she could still get excited with the right stimulation. I knew we could work together.

Skye had what by all accounts was a good job: at 46, she had risen to a middle management position in the civil service, earning enough to manage a lifestyle she described as comfortable, with funds for professional development, as well as excellent benefits, pension and vacation allowance. In the career industry, we call those perks "golden handcuffs." You feel trapped because things are too good to leave, even when you aren't happy.

Skye had actually been exploring career change on her own for several years before she was referred to me. She'd used her professional development budget to take courses in a number of areas she thought she might be interested in, and had read a lot of books and done a lot of exercises. At one point she said to me, "This had better not be another *What Colour is My Damn Parachute?* deal because I've had it up to here with that!" I told her that, while I respected that important book (there is no expletive in its actual title, by the way…), we'd do our own thing, and I'd need her to let me trust my instincts on what that would be each time we met.

Which courses or exercises did Skye like? None of them. What sparked an interest? Zip. Zilch. Nothing. And my asking was only making her more testy. Skye hadn't just lost touch with what made her happy; she had lost touch with any belief that she had ever been happy, or ever could be. And I knew we had to get that back before she would let any of our work have any effect on her.

I asked her to choose four hours worth of theoretically fun activities to add to each week. I believe "Are you crazy?" was Skye's first response.

"Maybe, but I'd still like you to try this," was my reply. She didn't know what to do! I gave her about a dozen suggestions (movies; yoga; cooking class; walking group; a date with her husband; time with her nieces; a book club; a massage; dancing; window shopping; a facial; concert; rollerblading...) and told her to pick any three. "But I don't have time – I barely have time to see you! I'm overworked already!"

> When you are disconnected from yourself and don't know what to do, having more time just makes you more disconnected because the pain of the not knowing becomes that much more nagging in a world without distraction.

Ah, that old chestnut. Most people who are not loving what they are doing but can neither imagine a better future nor take action to leave say that they can't change the way they are living because they don't have enough time. They fantasize about winning the lottery not so much because they want a luxurious lifestyle but because they want the simple freedom of expanses of time to do whatever they are not doing now – or more to the point, just to *not* be doing what they *are* doing now. Yet, nowhere in my experience have I seen huge expanses of time serve as catalysts to positive change. On the contrary, I've seen more people become paralyzed, bored and stuck. When you are disconnected from yourself and don't know what to do, having more time just makes you more disconnected because the pain of the not knowing becomes that much more nagging in a world without distraction.

Lest you think I am opposed to solitude, sabbaticals or other forms of 'free' time, let me say that I am strongly in favour of all of them as a great gift to the self once we have engaged in a dialogue with our inner knowing and have some idea of for what purpose and in what ways we would like to structure our open space. When absent structure comes alongside absent connection to self, most of us don't find that connection – rather we flounder desperately, too many options making us choose none and go nowhere.

Ever heard the expression "Wanna get something done - give it to a busy person"? There is a reason that cliché is still in circulation: it's true most of the time. Honestly want to know yourself and take some steps toward change? Add them on to the schedule you already have; piggyback them on activities you have already habituated; connect with other people (supportive friends; discussion or networking groups; professional or community associations; coaches, counsellors or other guides) and trust the change will come in motion rather than in stillness. And when it comes, you can enjoy your stillness in gratitude rather than panic.

It took two sessions of cajoling but Skye did add some new activities to her schedule. And for two more sessions she just told me how pointless she thought they were. "Humour me," I said. And she stuck with it – if only, we both realized, for the opportunity to prove me wrong. Fortunately, it didn't come to that. One day, she came to see me with a happy story of laughing so hard at a charity bowling event with some co-workers that she almost peed her pants. Skye remembered what she had forgotten: she likes to laugh. She likes her co-workers. And she loves laughing as part of her workday. The beginnings of something we could both work with…

Skye was able to succeed at making some of the changes she liked because we didn't wait for her to feel and see differently before she *acted* differently and we didn't wait for her Super 7 ticket to win for her to simply take the structured time she needed to create change. Her life already had two basic categories: (1) working at her job and (2) dreading working at her job. We simply added a third category for two lunch hours during category one and two evenings during category two, which became Category (3) doing enjoyable things unrelated to her job. You laugh; this sounds so simple, it's almost silly. Yet how many people do you know who live in categories one and two for years without being able to break out? Indeed, without it even occurring to them to do so? Skye took the first critical step to reconnecting to hope and promise, and then took many more.

Once Skye was re-opened to the idea that her life could in any way be different, it was possible for us to look at the specifics of *how* she would like it to be different. The quality of life she wanted, not the new job title she might have.

Each time we talked, Skye just kept coming back to an inner knowing that something was missing: her life was *busy*, but not *full*. And that's a clue that she wasn't living in a values-based way. There are only a few things in life I would say I know for sure, and this is one of them:

Living our values makes us feel full.

Living without values makes us feel stuffed but empty, like bingeing on junk food and regretting it after. No matter how many people, experiences or things we have in our lives, we can never get enough of what we don't really want, so we are always hungry for more.

Over the years, I've watched a lot of people enjoy radical reinventions in search of authenticity and the blissful paradox of "passionate contentment" that comes with it. Former 9-to-5 'security addicts' who've become home-based entrepreneurs. The client who left her glossy, hardwood-floored downtown apartment for a hardcore, down home experience of hobby farming: she moved from hiding the cat from the strata council to caring for cats, dogs, horses, sheep and goats! Others who left fast-paced corporate careers to become professional students, nurses, writers and artists... and writers and artists who learned to manage their careers, charge what they were worth and enjoy entrepreneurial as well as creative success.

This is the kind of change Skye thought she wanted: big, bold, sweeping... to undergo something akin to a religious conversion or physical transformation and to come out recognizable only to herself. Yet I know without a doubt that as many *lives* – maybe even many more lives – can be improved just as meaningfully by smaller changes: less sweeping but equally impactful, and I invited Skye to try some baby steps and see where they might take her first.

You'll recall that when we started together, Skye was seriously stressed and quite convinced that she needed to find a whole new career in order to bring balance to her life – pretty understandable feelings when you consider that she routinely worked from 7am to 7 or 8pm, grabbed lunch at her desk, and that a good weekend was one in which she only went in to work for "a few" hours.§ Once we had her leaving work before 6pm several nights each week – even laughing now and then! – she regained enough perspective to consider an introspective look at her values.

I gave her a values survey I use which filters about 120 possible values, prompting the user to rank the relative importance of each one in a personal way. Then we spent a couple of hours looking at her Top twenty, teasing out a few that the exercise did not offer but which were clearly important to her, and later reducing that down to the eight values she would choose to give priority expression in her daily life.

And they were, in order of importance to her:

1. Creativity
2. Leadership
3. Multi-Dimensional Health & Wellness
4. Compassion & Social Justice
5. Laughter, Fun & Adventure
6. Friendship & Community
7. Solace
8. Stability & Security

Where Skye had once been the creative force behind many projects and the head of some strong teams, her two most recent promotions had moved her more and more into a world of budgets, regulations, compliance and reporting. The increasingly pressured and politicized environment and many new aspects of the job – especially cost projections and endless tracking of expenditures – overshadowed the enjoyment she had once experienced at clarifying a vision and supporting a team to bring it to life. Clearly, that would have to change, yet she found herself thinking that maybe she no

---

§ I know some of you are reading that and thinking, "So? I work those hours and I don't have a problem. I love what I do!" And I believe you. Unlike a lot of people in my profession, I do not presume that work must not occupy more than 50 hours per week before my client is diagnosed as a workaholic and sent to a 12-Step Group. On the contrary, I think balance looks different in each life and my only criterion is the happiness of the individual. Skye's experience was not one of passionate commitment to an all-consuming project. Rather, her passion was being consumed by a job that was strangling her. And that needed to change.

longer wanted to leave her employer entirely: after much discussion, it was clear that the security of a government job and the opportunity to make a difference in creating programs which offered outreach and support to less fortunate members of society mattered to Skye very deeply. On reflection, it seemed like quitting her job would be throwing the baby out with the bathwater. Happily, the wellness piece was already improving with time for friends and exercise, and if she could get off work on time and stop working weekends, Skye was confident she could get the solace she needed to feel like she was living all of her core values.

In simply clarifying her values and making space to consider change, Skye already made the biggest change of all: a shift in consciousness. She felt stronger and more focused at work and her no-exceptions basic self care policy created incentive and structure to begin taming her workload. Day by day, focused on building a life that mostly worked for her instead of mostly living at work, Skye found herself feeling healthier, stronger and able once again to genuinely enjoy the parts of her job that appealed to her interests and drew on her natural gifts. That's when the universe stepped in to give her a little help. (Dontcha just love it when that happens? And it always does if you give it a chance.)

Downsizing. Who knew there could be a precious gift hidden in a package like that? And *package* is the operative word... the offer of a "voluntary termination" package gave Skye a real choice about her job. The choice to leave was one she had always had, really, but it was certainly more attractive this day than the day before now that it came with a generous financial incentive. After crunching the numbers and thinking seriously about it, Skye concluded that the buyout wasn't right for her at the time and she would stay where she was. That didn't mean she didn't experience change: on the contrary, she quickly noticed improvement in how she felt about each day at work. Small irritations were less irritating; other people's stresses less penetrating. Aware at every moment that she had chosen and charted her own course, Skye was able to respond to whatever was going on around her in a positive, confident and empowered way.

And from there it just got better: in all the restructuring that accompanied many people's acceptance of buyout packages, an opportunity arose for job descriptions to be rewritten – and Skye was ready to seize it! She took on the task of creating the job she would like to have, drafting

> **Sometimes the change you seek can't be had by focusing on the world outside your employer's walls...looks like you want to negotiate the job.**

a proposal and rationale, and we worked together to create her dream job description. Because she made it easy for them to say yes, her supervisors let her move into the role exactly as we had written it. Soon Skye's hours of juggling numbers dropped to less than 20% of what they once were, with all of that extra time devoted to her specialization – and her passion – developing proposals, facilitating brainstorming meetings, team building and project stewardship.

The takeaway? When you know that you have choices, when you open to trying new things and talking to new people, when you move yourself to a place where you can smile and laugh – even for no particular reason – amazing things begin to happen. Your fresh experiences bring a fresh perspective; your fresh perspective brings even fresher experiences... and you've started the process of turning a vicious cycle into a virtuous one.

Almost every great thinker in the world, whether philosopher, theologian or epistemologist has offered some version of the wisdom that we change the world by changing ourselves. Skye was able to change her experience of her job by changing her experiences outside her job, which in turn changed the way she experiences everything. From that place she was free to make any choice: she could stay at her job but mind it less; change jobs within her organization; leave the organization… the sky(e) was the limit!

Sometimes the change you seek can't be had by focusing on the world outside your employer's walls: maybe you've already maximized every ounce of family/friends/exercise/nutrition/ community involvement/civic action/ personal growth/quality sleep you can and the job still isn't doing it for you as-is, but the pros of staying still outweigh the cons when you consider leaving and starting over. (You'd want to be sure that those pros really are that good and you're not just succumbing to a natural fear of stepping out of your comfort zone, of course.) Assuming you've taken an incisive look at what's going on for you in your job and come up confident that it needs tweaking and you can, in fact, be the tweaking agent, then it looks like you want to negotiate the job.

One of the best negotiators I ever worked with was a young man named Abbas. Abbas was 26 years old when he came to be a client, three years into his second career-level job out of university, working in a hybrid role made up of promotions, events and client relationship management for a large business association. Abbas's job involved prepping collaterals and logistics for major trade shows, conferences and networking events, and providing back-end service to businesses and related associations who were exhibiting, speaking or doing other promotions at the events his association sponsored or ran in-house. He had a database of over 15,000 contacts and juggled as many as 200 emails and 50 phone calls a day, and most days he genuinely loved it.

His eyes lit up when he told me about getting some hotelier to bump up the booth footprint from 10 x 10 to 12 x 15 to give platinum level sponsors seating areas at their exhibits, or figuring out how to ship some

3D interactive technology exhibit from one convention centre to another for overnight set-up. I mean, the guy actually got excited about things like titanium pop-ups, special pricing on full bleed banners and logoware. (And thanks to Abbas, I now actually know what all of those words mean!) Every day held creativity, challenge and dramatic problem-solving, snatching victory from the jaws of defeat – and Abbas loved every minute of it. He also knew that jobs like this were few and far between and he was already working for one of the most reputable associations of its kind.

His relationship to a few of his co-workers was less loving, however. Abbas felt that as low man on the totem pole and the only service person on a team of managers, directors and sales people, his needs were often overlooked and his role disrespected. He didn't mind being the go-to guy for every client crisis; in fact, he really enjoyed being someone on whom clients depended and who could step up and deliver under pressure. He just didn't think that some of the pressure was really necessary.

In particular, Abbas felt that many of the sales people on his team made promises to clients in a way that put unrealistic and foolish demands on his schedule, and that management often solved problems in a knee-jerk way which just created new problems down the line, usually by a failure to communicate around root causes or planned remedies until after staff were stepping all over each other, and on days like that he thought seriously of leaving. (I'm sure no one reading this book has ever had that problem, of course.) Yet he was torn because moving on would mean giving up his prime placement in his field and all the creativity he so enjoyed; moving up wouldn't be an option until someone retired. Given the demographics in his organization, he had the best chances of moving up in two to three years by staying where he was.

Abbas was aware that his representation of himself as the guy who can handle anything was at once responsible for his having achieved so much at such a young age and also cursing him with a reputation as 'Mr. No-Problem-Easygoing-Always-Gets-the-Job-Done-So-We-Don't-Have-to-Consider-His-Feelings.' Under the heading of "We Teach People How to Treat Us," three years into delivering a lesson plan that obviously wasn't serving his peace of mind or his advancement, Abbas realized he had a remedial class he needed to deliver and he came to me for guidance.

I talked to him about how he responds when he his asked to do something out of the ordinary. "Asked?" he said. "Nobody asks. They just dump it on my desk."

"Okay," I said. "What do you do when they dump?"

"I do the work."

"Do you say anything?> Ask questions? Talk about timeline?"

"No," said Abbas, "I'm at the bottom; I have to get it done."

"It seems to me that you're the one creating the expectations here," I said. "My assumptions as a manager have always been that it is my job to understand my staff's workload and to create an environment where they can do their best work. I have also always asked them to push back if I ever pushed too hard. Has your immediate supervisor ever said anything about your workload or how you can give feedback?"

Abbas wrinkled up his face as he said, "Sure, but that's just lip service. Everyone says their door is always open but in real life they never even leave it ajar! We all know we just have to get things done."

"Hmm," I said, "I don't know anything for sure except that by your own estimation, your boss really has no way of knowing how much work you have on your desk or how long it takes you to get a certain type of task done. Correct?"

"He *should* know," said Abbas.

"How *can* he know if you don't tell him?" I countered.

"He used to do my job," Abbas mumbled.

Before I could say, "How long ago and in what incarnation?" Abbas said "Okay, okay. I'll talk to him. What do I say?"

I suggested that the next time some surprise workload finds its way onto his desk, Abbas should go to whomever gave it to him, tell them he will need X hours to complete it, that he has Y hours of work to complete in Z number of available hours, and ask which of the projects he has right now should take priority. That will gently put his workload into a context and create some awareness around what he does and how he does it. As Phase Two, I advised Abbas to start making discussion of project scope, timelines and deadlines a regular part of sales and operations meeting agendas.

Though we knew nothing would change overnight, it seemed important to slowly educate his team about what he actually did — without scolding or complaining. Just a matter-of-fact presentation. Each conversation about timelines and priorities became an indirect negotiation of how his time would be used, and how his contributions would be managed and recognized.

After a couple of weeks reporting that he had managed to get some of his points made in conversations with higher ups but that he saw no other progress, Abbas excitedly delivered the news that his boss had actually come to him with a project and asked him how long it would take to do. He was being acknowledged as someone with a schedule to keep, with other projects to manage! Exactly what he wanted! And the acknowledgement kept happening, slowly but surely, week after week. The more Abbas believed he was in fact deserving of respect and that it was possible even people substantially older than he would respect him, the more he acted like someone to be respected, and the more respect he received. See how the virtuous cycle becomes self-generating? Thinking and feeling, then strategically acting in alignment with that thinking and feeling, then allowing ourselves to receive the new outcome – and celebrate!

Beginning to feel more self-respect and dreaming bigger about his future, Abbas asked if we could spend some time envisioning where his job might go after a few years. "What should my long term goals be?" I told him what I would tell anyone who asked that question: I support you to ask and answer your own questions. You wouldn't want me to set your goals for you. A little back and forth resistance, playing the "But I don't know" game, and then Abbas said, "Okay, promise you won't laugh? Never mind – I know you won't. But you can if you want to."

(I love the way that grown ups of all ages turn into precious, innocently vulnerable children when they get close to talking about something really BIG.)

"Alright, the thing is… Well… I'm a really good Ultimate player." Pause. "You know, the game where girls and guys play on a big field with a Frisbee and lots of running and an honour code?" he said on one great rush.

I confess, I had absolutely no idea what he was talking about but it sounded like a good thing in general and a great thing to him, so I said with all the enthusiasm I could muster, "You're really good! That's wonderful!" and waited for him to elaborate.

"Well," said Abbas, "I want to be able to work three days a week, ideally, maybe sometimes four, but definitely not five in the summer months," he said breathlessly, "so I can travel to play more Ultimate. And I need to figure out how to get the time off."

I gotta say: I've been doing this a long time, helped a lot of clients negotiate flex time, but doing so to play Frisbee, however extreme or evolved a version of the sport it may be, was a new one on me. I cleared my throat and told myself to have an open mind. "Okay, are there any other three to five year goals we should fit in to this picture?" I asked.

"Now that you mention it, I'd like to take on more responsibility. I want to learn more about managing accounts and not just servicing them. I think that some of the reason I am not respected at work is that I am not directly involved in generating any of the revenue. If I proved that I could do that, they would take me more seriously," Abbas concluded.

I tell clients to dream big: I owe it to them to get on board all the way when they do. It is my firm belief that a key reason why many people do not achieve their goals (that's the 5% of you who create space in your lives to consciously *set* goals) is that the goals are little more than 'To Do' lists – transactional, modest, and uninspiring. Big dreams get us up in the morning. They scare us, of course, but they also elevate and enrich us and give as much energy as they expend. Small goals feel like little more than self-prescribed obligations; dreams are expansive, generative. They feed us so we feed them. We procrastinate about tasks; we don't tend to about dreams. The bigger the better, I say.

And so began three sessions looking at new goals Abbas had set for his work/life, his rationale for why he wanted both shorter work weeks and more responsibility at the same time, some research into and analysis of company goals which would be congruent and/or in conflict with his personal ones, and drafting a point-by-point proposal which formally requested and gave evidence supporting mutual interests being served by giving him more training, sales responsibilities, and a six day week in peak trade show periods of Fall and Spring to allow for a three-four day week in Summer, when events were naturally slower, anyway.

Abbas requested a meeting with his immediate supervisor and the division director – I suggested seeing them both at once so he could make his pitch himself rather than having someone else take it up the food chain for him. No one else would have the interest or the ability to make his case with the passion and sincerity he would bring to it. We had anticipated and planned for every possible objection, and role played responses from every angle. Abbas went into the meeting *ready*. More importantly, he went into it okay no matter what happened, saying the day before:

> I tell clients to dream big: I owe it to them to get on board all the way when they do...Big dreams get us up in the morning. They scare us, of course, but they also elevate and enrich us and give as much energy as they expend.

"Alanna, a month ago I would have said that I couldn't imagine staying in this job if I didn't get to do more interesting things and add some more spice to my life with more sport and adventure. But I have learned so much in this process of taking myself more seriously, seeing a bigger picture, putting this presentation together: this has been the kind of challenge I wanted to sink my teeth into. Whatever happens now, just knowing I stepped up is enough, at least for now. It's like you say – you can't always know if you are doing the right thing. Just try to have the right reasons and go from there. So that's what we'll do and it's a win no matter how it turns out."

The days don't get much better than that for me. Abbas's sincere confidence, gratitude and clarity warmed me in a way I can't even describe. Moments like that and I know I am in my dharma and I have the best job I could ever imagine for myself.

And you just know things had to work out for Abbas, right? Coming from that place, so centred in himself? His boss said he had showed a side of himself that they hadn't seen yet and they were impressed. They agreed to let him sit in on some key business development meetings and to work four Saturdays in February and March (peak trade show season) in exchange for four Fridays in July and August (peak Ultimate season – who knew?) on a trial basis, with a review in September to see how it had all worked out.

Beautiful! Golden! Lemonade!

Chapter 6

No Draft Picks, Just Many First Rounds:
Life as a Free Agent

The Free Agent life – so named for Daniel Pink's great book *Free Agent Nation* from the late 90s – is attracting many more people with each passing year. Many choose it to get away from something – ranging from their idiot former boss, 60-hour workweeks, milkrun business travel and the airless veal-fattening pen cubicles in which they work to a constant sense of restlessness, never being satisfied or 'done,' a malaise that sets in by 9:30 on Monday morning and worsens progressively until on Friday they are gasping for air and only barely catching their breath on Saturday before their case of the "Sunday Night Dreads" springs into action, usurping all hope of a restful sleep with its overwhelming angst and grief at the thought of going to work the next day…

I wish I made that stuff up and we could all decide I have a future writing daytime soap operas if I wanted (okay, I do!), but in fact those are just a few snippets of the heart-wrenching stories I have heard from hundreds of clients before they found the Free Agent path. However dispirited they may have felt when they took this turn, however, those who really embrace and succeed in Free Agency fairly quickly find a way to make it about going *toward* something: independence, service, community, social venture, balance, challenge, excellence, joy… Maslow's self actualization, of course, found in experiences of our highest human values.

Not to say that there are never grounds or uses for running away; sometimes that's just how we get our speed up to get going where we want to go. Like any survival instinct, it has its place. Thriving instincts are just better ways to live.

A few years ago, I ran a month-long web survey of Free Agents asking them what attracted them to Free Agency and what they loved best about their new path. I received several hundred, very detailed responses, this just a small sampling:

- "I chose this business as a way to control my own future. At the time I started it, it was difficult to obtain a job in my field. Rather than spend countless months doing stuff I was overqualified for or knock on doors begging people to hire me, I felt it would be better for my future to strike out on my own."

- "You can make a lot more money doing short contracts in IT. And I get bored easily. The combination of profit and variety made sense and 8 years in, I love it as much as I ever did. You have to get used to the uncertainty, not always knowing where the next cheque is coming from, but if you can have faith, it's a great life."

- "I was ready to be responsible for my own success."

- "I started my own consulting business after I was laid off from a large company. It was a matter of taking control of an unfortunate situation."

- "I like working in jeans and I don't like commuting: what more can you ask for?"

- "I'm a home-schooler. More specifically, I'm am un-schooler. We chose to leave city life and I can work from my home, communicating professionally with clients, while multi-tasking with my kids' lessons and housework. I can work late into the night or early in the morning – whenever I can catch an hour or two."

- "I am very efficient at time and task management and can accomplish a lot in just a few hours. It's preferable to be self-employed rather than stuck in an office committed to 40 hours per week with a lot of them just filling in time. Now, I get my full day's work done in 4-5 hours and then I think, 'What's today's adventure going to be?'"

- "I feel that big corporations won't be around for my future so I am creating my own."

- "No one would hire me in my specialty. They all thought I was too young. Any job I took would mean spending over half my time on stuff I don't like to do. Now I spend 90% of my time on work I really enjoy. I get more respect for the work I do. And I'm aging not just gracefully but profitably."

- "My wife has a demanding career which involves lots of travel. All I need is a phone and a computer with a high speed internet connection and I'm good to go. So I'm the big winner here because I get tons more hours with our kids, both my wife and I enjoy what we do, and our family has a great lifestyle."

You get the idea, right? There is no one story in all of this. But there are, appropriately, many stories of *freedom*, in one form or another, and of *agency* – as pro-activity, subject not object. Accountability and creativity.

Most of the Free Agents I have coached say that coping with their fear is without question the toughest thing they had to do to change their lives. One could say that fear is the toughest thing anybody deals with to make any kind of change and be right, of course. But Free Agents are doing something which no one in our culture has done in several generations.

> What makes this transition sing is a vision so strong that, once crystallized in your mind's eye, it's honestly like you've already done it. You are here, yes, but you are also there, wherever you are going...And when you get to that place, the here and there of your dream, you know it in your bones, literally in every cell and fibre of your being, you find that there simply cease to be any excuses that would stand in your way any longer.

Changing jobs means at least going to another "job" and you know what that is. Even choosing unemployment or buying a business has paths already forged you can walk. Retirement is also understood, with well-worn paths in a number of different directions. Free Agents are not just working without a net; they are most often working without role models. They are inventors and magicians every one of them, creating something new, making their life appear out of thin air.

What makes this transition sing is a vision so strong that, once crystallized in your mind's eye, it's honestly like you've already done it. You are here, yes, but you are also there, wherever you are going. Present and future at the same time because you have been there where it counts: on the inside. And when you get to that place, the here and there of your dream, you know it in your bones, literally in every cell and fibre of your being, you find that there simply cease to be any excuses that would stand in your way any longer. That doesn't mean that you never procrastinate or tell yourself a silly story anymore, nor that you never get scared or have doubts.

It means that your passion and purpose are so much stronger, their pull so seductive, the love you experience so grand and compelling, that these momentary slips when you forget how great you are and disconnect from your vision can only be short-lived. So while roadblocks pop up to say "I can't pitch to big companies until I have my own LCD projector and laser pointer" or "They won't take me seriously if I don't have a downtown corporate address" and "I'll never be able to concentrate with the kids running around," you just learn, quite organically, really, how to talk yourself through them and get back to the only truth that matters: you know what you want and you're already getting it.

The stories which follow are examples of exactly that: transforming narrative where clients learned how to edit the stories which were stopping them to create the stories in which they can be heroes.

One client, Tamara, a 46 year-old mother of two, had just come through the pretty successful start-up of a new home-based business as a web developer and is now in the expansion phase of pursuing bigger clients and following up on referrals and leads. It's both a critical and an exciting time and Tamara has been fortunate to receive lots of support, with multiple former colleagues and clients throwing business opportunities her way. Sounds like it's all sunshine and roses, right? Except, those golden moments, at least when they are just new and our confidence can still feel shaky, are often exactly when fear will come into play. In our most recent coaching session, Tamara unhappily reported having met just one of the five commitments she had made the previous week.

"I just don't know what got into me," Tamara said incredulously. "I've got a rainbow of golden opportunities smack dab in front of me, but stuff just keeps coming up at the worst possible times and getting in the way. I mean, you wouldn't believe the week I've had if I told you!"

Aware that the emergence of dramatic "cliché speak" often signals emotional blocking for many of us, even a slip backwards in time to a very young emotional age, I was careful to keep the smile out of my voice as I said, "Try me."

"Well," said Tamara, "First of all, that volunteer project *you* thought would be such a great networking opportunity has turned out to be an organizational nightmare. Even a simple task takes three phone calls and seven emails to pull off. I just got so tied up with all the logistical stuff that I didn't have time to email the client referral you sent me or to call back that lead I got from my dentist last week. And, then, when I went to the mall to find the thank you cards I wanted to send to the Board members who've been helping out with my project, there just wasn't anything suitable. I went to, like, five or six different card stores, but nothing was right. And, then, on top of that, I had to be home for the plumber! It just seems like the world is conspiring against me so I can't get my stuff done!"

(Note to all of us: when your thinking gets so distorted that you believe any part of the universe actually has the desire or even the spare energy to intentionally thwart you, it's a burning bush kind of sign that you're in fear. The feelings are understandable and valid, but the thinking behind them isn't. It's time to look within and get some perspective.)

I heard another "And then . . ." coming from Tamara and decided it was as good a time as any to jump into the fray.

"Let's recap: Last week you committed to sending two follow-up emails and making two first-contact telephone calls to potential clients, all of them referred to you by people you know. You also said you wanted to send five thank you cards, outline a proposal for a requested project expansion for an existing client, and RSVP to the barbecue fundraiser you were invited to attend. Of those commitments, you did outline the proposal, but didn't do the rest, correct?"

"Uh huh," came the reply.

Honesty and brevity. Good. "Okay, give me your worst case scenario estimate," I asked. "How long would it take you to write two emails, make two phone calls, fill out an RSVP card and sign and address five cards and envelopes?"

Tamara wasn't quite ready to answer the question as asked. "Um," she said, "I really wanted to do it, you know. I hate it that all my time got sucked up."

I don't give up that easily. "How long would it take?"

"Two hours at the outside," came Tamara's estimate.

"That seems pretty fair," I responded. "But this was a really hard week, and you maybe wanted to rough out the notes and proofread them before writing good copies; you probably even wanted to draft talking points before you made the calls. And there's getting to the post office, of course. Let's triple that and say six hours to be really safe."

"Yeah," Tamara relaxed a little. "I could definitely have done it if I'd had six extra hours."

"EXTRA hours for generating business?" I interjected incredulously. We both know you set that as a top three priority, not something for spare time, but we'll come back to that. For now I want to explore what was really going on for you that you didn't make it happen."

"I told you," Tamara said. "There were all those phone calls and emails and the plumber..."

"You just told me the calls and emails would take you six hours max. It's been eight days. You're a smart and talented woman, well able to multi-task. And this is work you have chosen for yourself, your business, your creation. I think we both know that what's going on for you is *not* logistical!"

"Yeah, but, you know, looking for the cards took almost a whole day and I couldn't even find anything," Tamara protested.

Uh oh. She was really far gone this time, I thought. "So in downtown Vancouver, population two million, retail sector 20 square blocks of stores, you're telling me not one in five – it was five right?" She nodded. "Not one of five card stores had thank you cards?"

"Okay, they HAD them," she said, her voice starting to show the hesitation that said even she knew she had stopped making sense a few miles back... and then, no, not yet. Back to resistance for another tour. "It's just that they were all Martha Stewart and flowery. They weren't RIGHT."

It's okay. We have time. We'll get there. "What about blank cards?" I tried. "Or nice, textured note paper?"

"They weren't right, either. Image is important. It's part of my brand," came Tamara's defense of her position.

"And the RSVP?" I asked, trying another tack. "You had a self-addressed return envelope, right? We're talking about checking a 'yes' box and licking the back flap. What happened there?"

Alas, it was going to be one of those gets-worse-before-it-gets-better sessions. Tamara replied: "You know, I've been thinking. I really don't like barbecued food. It all tastes the same – hickory-smoked, mesquite-charred everything! Nasty toxins in the charcoal... And I saw this documentary about how they make hamburger that was really scary. Did you know they add extra fat to the regular meat bits and..."

"Tamara," I interjected at last, "What does hamburger and barbecue sauce have to do with attending a networking event at the invitation of your biggest client?"

"But I don't like barbecues!" she cried, all the force of the four year-old self with whom I was now dialoging, complete with the pout. "I don't want to have to eat food I don't like!" All she needed was a foot stomp to complete the mental picture I had of her little girl self.

I smiled. "Tell me something we can both believe."

Tamara started to argue back but then stopped herself. I felt like I could actually see a penny dropping. She paused for a long time, truth and fiction wrestling in her mind, then finally said, "I don't belong there. Those people run corporations, not home offices. I'm nowhere near their league. I'll just say something stupid and then spill food down my shirt."

"Now I see the fear of barbecue sauce..." I replied. "Anything else?"

"I don't have anything to wear. I never know what to say. I hate shaking hands. And if I get even one of those jobs from these people, I'm going to have to work so hard. I'll have to keep going to these events, and keep doing bigger and bigger jobs and keep on..."

That sounded exhausting, and I told Tamara as much. I'd be tired, too, as would any of us, I think. Tamara was describing the classic, and all-too-common, triple whammy -- a dose of fear powerful enough to cause procrastination-as-a-way-of-life paralysis, keeping people stuck in ruts for months and even years:

1. Fear of Failure. (I'm not in their league; I won't fit in.)

2. Fear of Success. (I'll have to keep maintaining impossibly high standards.)

3. Fear of Fear. (I'm exhausted and overwhelmed and I'd do anything not to have to feel this way.)

When you are procrastinating, when you are self-sabotaging, when you are choosing not to pursue the attractive, viable opportunities you yourself have created, you are afraid. Period. It's not about time or money (though managing those well is helpful); it's not about food preferences

When you are procrastinating, when you are self-sabotaging, when you are choosing not to pursue the attractive, viable opportunities you yourself have created, you are afraid. Period.

(though we're all entitled to them); and it's certainly not about product availability (though I'm as selective in my personal tastes and brand integrity as the next person). It's fear.

When you acknowledge your emotions and both name and accept fear for what it is, you take away at lot of its power... after all, at least you've gotten past your fear of fear! One down, two to go.

Next, you need to recognize that, if you're going to deal in a straight-up, no denial, get-real-with-yourself way, you've got just two basic choices when it comes to fear: (1) Stay exactly where you are in life and never again try anything new for as long as you live – which is a valid choice and perfectly okay with me if it is genuinely something you want and you understand that it will take some fancy footwork on your part to remain static in the face of all the changes that are guaranteed to happen around you. (2) Go through the fear to get to the other side – which is, by the way, the real reason that the chicken crossed the road.

I'm assuming most of you are going to choose option two – regardless of how readily or skeptically you may regard my assertion that the only way out of fear is through it. Having acknowledged fear for what it is, you need to take it down to a manageable size. You won't get rid of it, but you can put your energy into your own empowerment instead of feeding your fear and, in so doing, cause your power to grow and your fear to shrink.

Some people do this with creative visualization, literally constructing a mental representation of their fear (maybe a tricky Tasmanian Devil or a quaking, Cowardly Lion) and then slowly shrinking it. Others use relaxation techniques and meditative breathing to lessen their physical experience of anxiety and allow them to feel calmer, more capable. I also know working with a talented professional on some guided meditation can be a powerful boost to a lot of people.

Being pretty verbal in orientation myself, I usually opt to talk fear down. For example, I helped Tamara to talk down one of the fears she expressed above as follows:

"So, you're not in the corporate executive league, huh?" I clarified.

"It's not just executives; it's directors and politicians and lobbyists. People with huge careers compared to mine," she said.

"Wow." I knew what she meant. Almost any Free Agent with corporate clients has felt this; I certainly did in the early days. "So they're really successful and have lots of business experience – is that what I'm hearing?"

"Yes," Tamara said. "But not even just that. They know EVERYBODY. They're so connected. And they know way more than I do on pretty much any subject."

"So they're smarter than you?" I ventured, naturally expecting an argument.

"Yes, that's it exactly!" Tamara shot back – *actually grateful* that I had finally understood her problem is that she is not smart!?!

"Well," I said, always ready to do this another way if need be, "If they know more than you and they're smarter than you, I'd be inclined to trust their judgment then, wouldn't you?"

"Exactly," came Tamara's exasperated reply. "That's what I'm saying! They know so much more..."

"Yes," I stopped her. "And they invited *you*. They're smart; they know everyone; they can ask anyone they want to their party; and they picked you. So you must be in their league."

Tamara was not happy. She couldn't be right and happy at the same time, and at this moment she was going for right. "But I'm not..." she sputtered.

I was having none of it: I'm on the happy team. "Nope. Stop right there. You can't have it both ways. If they're smarter than you, they must be right. And I'm smart, too. And we're all saying you're ready. And the fact is when you look inside, you're smart, and you know you're ready, too. People who don't feel a least halfway ready never call me because they know I'm going to kick their ass into gear." At last, the laughter I was waiting for. Tamara was back. Sputtering still. Feeling a little fuzzy. But back. "So let's get on that RSVP, okay?" She nodded through her giggles.

Flash forward: RSVP sent; invitation accepted. Several additional conversations with fear anticipated between now and barbecue fundraiser date, but Tamara is game to have them. More personal and business growth to come. Such is Free Agent life.

It's not easy to deal with fear, but it is *simple*. Too often we confuse hard with complicated, and then we feel the need to add all the complicating layers to prove ourselves right. Simply, you can deal with fear any time you are willing to work through these four steps (and three of them are just in your head, capable of instantaneous shift in consciousness if you will allow it):

1. Accept that some measure of fear will always be a part of your life.

2. Acknowledge and name specific fears as they arise.

3. Refuse to feed your fear and use your highest, most rational and adult self to talk fear down to a manageable size, and, if necessary, get someone else to help you do this.

4. Do what you want to do, using your fear as a stepping stone instead of a stumbling block.

The good news is you can do this for yourself any time you need to. The bad news is, in Free Agent life, you'll need to... a lot... more often the bigger your dreams for your work/life become. But, then again, I think dreaming big and going for it is pretty good news, too, don't you?

Free Agency is often chosen out of a desire for a certain lifestyle, a particular way of doing work/life and of being in the world. Not everyone gets it. Another of the biggest challenges my Free Agent clients face comes in the form of the many and various people who step up trying to pull them off their path, along with the opportunity and necessity of redefining and/or recommitting to their lifestyle vision as success brings competing demands.

Allow me to illustrate with the story of Maya, a thirtysomething environmental geologist who worked on remediation projects (in the sort of plain English that I understand, so hopefully you will, too, that means that when governments or companies find out there is toxic gunk in the land or water where people want to live or build, Maya oversees the analysis and planning for how to get the gunk out so it will be safe for human habitation. I think I did that pretty well: Maya would be proud...) After a number of years working for a multinational engineering firm, and a couple of years working for an environmental protection-oriented NGO, Maya decided to go out on her own.

She had lots of relationships to build on – she managed the perfect Free Agent hat trick, in fact: becoming an independent, getting hired back as a consultant to her former employer, and setting – and getting – a substantially higher rate! Maya enjoyed the challenges of her work and liked the variety and balance she enjoyed by having clients in diverse sectors and multiple projects going on at the same time. She joined a small 'pod' of colleagues with complimentary skills sets and specialties and they quickly began referring work to one another.

While she liked the work, Maya began feeling as though she hadn't been clear enough in setting the intention for how she wanted to do that work. With so many old relationships still involved and project deadlines heating up, she felt she wasn't doing the work differently enough to satisfy her newly clarified values – a common occurrence as we find our way and raise our standards for living. (I often say that I encourage my clients to lower, not raise, their tolerance for negative stress – different from challenge or overcoming fear, this is the stuff that erodes capacity – so they will notice where they are out of their own integrity and make changes sooner.)

The actual transition into Free Agency had gone much more smoothly than she had ever dreamed; Maya's turbulence came when she found that her boundaries had gone from uncertain to fuzzy to 'um, boundary, what boundary?' and that is the point at which she called me. People she had worked with in one context, and who themselves continued to labour in a very 'billable hours' driven culture, often had expectations of her that she found very hard to get around. If they were working twelve hours a day, why wasn't she? If clean-up efforts would continue unabated over weekends to expedite project completion, shouldn't she be available to consult? If a client was prepared to pay time and a half for hours over eight in a day and double time for hours over 40 in a week, why wouldn't she just jump at the chance to rake in the dough?

And, truth be told, under the heading of 'we teach people how to treat us,' Maya admitted that for the first eight to twelve months in her new practice, that's exactly what she did. A bit fearful that work would not always flow in as abundantly as it did right away, $12,000 in start-up expenses for her incorporation, laptop, PDA and software licenses, and a new car in the mix, she had wanted to bring in as much revenue as she could as quickly as possible. Nothing wrong with that: we could have just planned for it, prepared clients for the idea that her initial accessibility was a special circumstance, this time only, alerted them that in the Fall (or Spring or second year or whatever), her business plan called for a certain availability. Now we had some unlearning to do, both for Maya and her clients.

We set about defining the experience of her work that Maya wanted to have – starting, as I always do, from the place that work is love made visible. So what did she love? And what did she want to see and be seen? Maya concluded that the best parts of her work were the initial client meetings, defining scope, doing proposals, and getting various members of the team on the same page with respect to timelines, parameters, technical specifications, community consultation and the like. She enjoyed being a mentor or resource person to her more junior colleagues as well. We both noted that, when we compared this description of what she loved to the lion's share of what she was doing, there was quite a disconnect. A lot of the work that came her way was after a proposal had been scoped or even accepted, and she was doing the technical heavy lifting while someone else built client relationships.

> **The reason to hire someone to help you focus and be congruent is precisely because there will be days when urgencies and pressures make you forget what you know, what you have already decided.**

That kind of mismatch had two implications for life and revenue: (1) Maya wasn't experiencing nearly as much joy as she wanted in her work, thus she was missing out on the energizing potential a meaningful career can have and just getting tired; that fatigue would soon be seen by her clients and could affect her reputation and sales. No matter what anyone tells you about short term cashflow, it is almost never a good idea to do work that you don't enjoy. Not even for money. (2) Because she wasn't meeting clients, she... well, wasn't meeting clients! Each time she took work on someone else's project instead of creating one of her own, she perpetuated the arrangement because the repeat business would go to her colleague as well, and she was not building tools, templates or capacity for the future. It was time to take the risk of not earning for a few days or even weeks so that she could create the kind of earning that she really wanted to do.

We decided on a 60-day plan to get her to that point. The timeframe would allow her to meet current commitments and go hard at her schedule to put away some cash to cover what we cautiously estimated could be as long as two months before she landed a full project of her own. (Two months is actually a pretty short timeline for generating substantial new business, but Maya had a strong network and track record to build on – this wasn't a 'cold' start...) Things were going along just fine when she was offered two additional projects from within her pod which would tie her up for as many as 90 days past our proposed timeline. She called me with the news, nervously trying to talk me into saying it was a good idea.

The reason to hire someone to help you focus and be congruent is precisely because there will be days when urgencies and pressures make you forget what you know, what you have already decided. My job in these situations is to hold the vision. If the vision changes, I hold the new one. If it hasn't changed, I don't buy the story, no matter what it is. Clients still make their own choices – I just shine the light where they asked me to shine it when they were thinking mindfully, and, if they move off course, they at least do so consciously.

So I asked Maya what about her goals for her practice and her life had changed? "Well," came her response, "David has some really good ideas about how we can use this company as a reference to get a contract with their sister company next year."

"That tells me about David's goals for his practice, one of which is to keep subcontracting to you because you are good at what you do. Where are your goals in this?" I asked.

"Well," she started again, "David has always been really good to me and I like working with him a lot."

"I'm glad you like David," I said. "But working for David instead of putting out your own RFPs and having him work for you means that he does the parts of the project you love and you do the parts of the project you tolerate. Unless you can tell me that you have learned to enjoy the soil analysis more this week than last week? Or that David is actually going to do all the grunt work this time and let you build the client relationship? Are there elements I am missing?"

"Sometimes you are not easy to like," Maya said.

"Like schmike! As long as you can still love me – and more importantly love your *practice* – when we're all done," I countered, "I can sleep just fine knowing you're miffed at me today." And so Maya recommended the work to a colleague instead and told David she hoped to have a project on which they would collaborate again next quarter. We got through the rest of the 60 day wind down unscathed and Maya set to work in earnest on her business plan, proposal template, and first few business development meetings. She was excited, energized, hopeful... and, of course, after two full weeks without a single billable hour, absolutely terrified.

Naturally it was the scariest day to date when the next call came, this one from one of her former employers. They were offering her an elevated version of her old job back: more consultation and development of junior consultants – just the stuff she loved – and a salary increase of about 30% which would come close to equaling her earning potential in solo private practice. (Did I mention it's my job to hold the vision?)

"I am flabbergasted," said Maya when she phoned me.

"Really? I'm barely surprised," I replied.

"Oh right, like you knew the firm would call?" she sputtered.

"Not the firm, no. But someone, yes. That's how this works – we are given opportunities to decide what we want, to affirm our intentions, to give us a chance to recommit, show our mettle, or possibly even choose differently. And they come when we need them. When you're not feeling overwhelmed you know that," I reminded her. "So which kind of opportunity is this?"

"How am I supposed to know?" she started, then took another tack. "Alright, I guess I do know. I don't want to have a job again. I want to work for myself. Contracts are one thing, employment is another."

"Does that mean decision made?" I asked, not quite sure I heard affirmation in her voice.

"Well, maybe I could talk them into a contract," came the reply – ah, that was the question I heard.

"Maybe you could, Maya," I responded. "If I remember correctly, though, these were the very people who had you working nights and weekends – and didn't they even promise a client a report of some kind on Boxing Day last year? When you pointed out the date, they grudgingly moved the deliverable from December 26 to December 27 – not exactly the work/life balance card, I'm thinking. So unless your mission and vision changed over the weekend..."

Alright, alright!" Maya yelled into the phone. "I hate this! It would be so much better if that hadn't called. Now I'm going to spend every day until I have positive cashflow again wondering if I made the wrong decision, if I should have accepted, if I can call them back and change my mind."

"If you're going to do that, you should just accept. Spending every day in doubt is the same thing. It's time to decide who you really are and what you really want."

Silence on the other end of the phone. Long silence. I waited. (Actually, I put the kettle on for tea. Cordless headsets are very good for this purpose; I can hang on a long time if I have to.)

"I want to work from home, for myself, on projects of my choosing!" Maya said finally. Then, her voice stronger: "And I want to sleep before midnight every night and in my own bed as often as possible because I send someone else to the work site and I stay in the city to liaise with clients and keep everything together. And I want to do community consultation!"

"I'm sold. Are you? Really?"

"I think so," Maya said.

"Really?"

"Yes!"

"So what are you going to do today?" I asked.

"Tell the firm no thank you and get my ass in gear to get a paying client!" she laughed. Sounded just right to me. And you know that client wasn't too long in coming, right?

So, whether you are living or contemplating Free Agency or just interested in bringing some more freedom to your experience of a regular job, how do you know what success looks like for you? And where did that image come from? How do you know when you are on the right track, when you're doing well? How do you know when one thing is "done" and it's time to move on to the next? Values-driven work/life often means moving away from external yardsticks and traditional forms of validation toward something that is more personal and that we have to make up (and frequently remake and recommit to) as we go along.

Success is often measured in terms of career and business, and within those areas, usually in units of dollars and clients and caseloads. And those are perfectly valid measures – for what they can tell us. What we too often forget, of course, is that they can only tell us some things, and they may leave out entirely some of the most important things.

Generally, the first Free Agent success is the first client, maybe only after which comes the first paying client, then the first big client, first referral client, and first repeat business from any of the above. Eventually, however, all those firsts run out. Then what? Well, once you're on seconds and thirds, it's usually about refining the systems to do the same things better, more quickly, less expensively, more profitably and with fewer mistakes. These are positive and perfectly valid goals. But a fuller, more holistic approach seeks a larger context, one in which your work is a reflection of your person, your values, your purpose and your desired quality of life.

Maya set the intention of growing her client base and revenues *in conjunction* with growing a balanced approach to her life – not one and then the other but rather the two in harmony. Not easy. But so worth it! No matter how much work was on her plate, Maya made a commitment to certain minimum levels of self care and certain maximum levels of work. For example: while her goal was eight hours of sleep per night, she set six as the minimum for busier periods. She sought to work out six days per week yet gave herself the flexibility to cut that down to three – and no less! – when needed. Food? The hard and fast rule was eating four times per day and none of it fast food, with the gesture toward the ideal being her concerted effort to cook whole foods at least three times per week, the loftovers taking care of many meals. And friends! So important and so easily lost in many of our hectic lives. Maya made a standing date to see each of her closest friends once a month as her minimum and set up a private blog where they could all fill each other in on what was going on in their lives more often. They generally saw each other more frequently than that, but setting the monthly date was a help in peak times and communicated the intention that people were important.

And the work itself? Her goal was to invest 90% of her time in contracts under her own company and to bill 50 hours per week and work 65 through the end of her second year, down to 40 billable and 50 worked in year three and a ratio of 35 to 40 in year four when she felt she would have enough brand to more substantially increase her rates and cut down on the non-billable time it took to secure new contracts. Tracking, monitoring, we'd see how she would do and revisit this regularly. Balance isn't perfection: it's a good faith effort, regular steps in the right direction, doing your best in context without letting the context overtake your best intentions and judgment.

Free Agents are teaching our entire culture that work, no matter how good we are at it or how much good we might do with it, is not a life. Success is ultimately in the living.

Chapter 7

Employee to Entrepreneur to Enterprise... Oh My!

The process of becoming yourself, of awakening your audacity and dreaming a bigger dream than you have ever allowed yourself before, is delicious exhilaration – for the one becoming, yes, but equally so for those of us privileged to bear witness. My practice has always included working with entrepreneurs, both emerging and established, and it brings me great joy to be able to serve their visions. Entrepreneurs are exciting and excitable: they grab onto ideas and run with them, full tilt, no thought but making it to the end zone... which is a tremendous gift most of the time.

Occasionally, as they make their headlong touchdown play, they suddenly become aware of the expectations of the roaring crowds, or the six or eight defensive players from the other team heading straight for them, and they briefly take their head out of the game. Naturally, that's exactly where a good coach comes in (...and this brings us to the end of the football metaphor interlude because we've now exhausted my knowledge of the game!)

Like Free Agency, unless you grew up in a family business, entrepreneurship involves stepping way out of familiar territory to chart an entirely new course, learning to tolerate feeling like the ground is shifting under you and finding your centre of balance within you instead of somewhere out in the world.

This chapter explores two stories: one a transition from employment to entrepreneurship; the second a larger leap from entrepreneurship to a true enterprise, embracing Michael Gerber's oft-quoted idea that you're not really in *business* until you have enough systems in place that the operation makes money whether you are there or not. Business is tough enough; living in conscious alignment with your values every day is even tougher. Running a consciously values-driven business, a social venture? I stand completely in awe. When you experience the stories of the following clients, I predict you will, too.

When I began working with Meredith, I knew that we would do great things together. I liked her immediately; fortunately, the feeling was mutual, and we developed an instant rapport as we found ourselves finishing each other's sentences from the get-go. She was already the kind of woman who would succeed if she chose to no matter what she did: smart, articulate, beautiful in a gentle, unassuming way, yet also determined in an assertive and daring way.

So why did she even call me, you might ask? If it's not clear from the other chapters by now (or if you're dipping and dabbling into the book in whatever order you choose), my clients tend to be people who have been blessed with considerable gifts and have mastered many of the arts of using them. There is no deficit or dysfunction here: the work is about actualizing human potential. And Meredith knew that she could do more of what she wanted and be more of herself if she got some outside perspective, a few fresh ideas, a little strategy… and some help dealing with her fears of success so that she would, in fact, "choose to" live the life she imagined for herself. Yup, that's what I said: fears of *success*.

We all know – experientially and intuitively – that it is common for people at all stages of life to fear failure. Being vulnerable, putting ourselves out there, and possibly not measuring up, being found wanting… we know what it feels like to want to avoid something, even if it's something we want very much, to avoid the risk that we might fail. What fewer of us realize is that we can be just as afraid of success – often in the very same instance – paralyzing ourselves with damned if we do/damned if we don't scenarios.

Meredith had left her job as a junior public relations consultant about a year and a half before we started working together. She had been grossly underpaid and underappreciated for what she had been doing, but was a strategic enough thinker to realize that it was a good move for her to suck it up in that company for a few years because they had been around for decades, weathered at lot of industry ups and downs, and would teach her the ropes in a pretty short period of time: PR Bootcamp, we later came to call it.

When Meredith sat down with me for the first time, she had just landed a substantial contract with a $5M/year corporation, a small client compared to the accounts she had handled in her previous firm but a very big deal for her small business, and she had made the very bold move of hiring an assistant to help her with research and project coordination. She was excited, happy, looking for an edge to help her speed up this steep growth curve and get to the next level.

We talked about her 3-5 years goals (downtown offices; six or seven people working under her; a well-deserved reputation for delivering value and results that drew larger and more substantial clients to her each year), her strengths (quick thinking, creativity, well-tended relationships in media and communications, thoroughness, integrity), and her strong desire to work with the right kind of people – as she put it, not just spin doctoring to clean up the corporate image of any company who could pay, but more of a naturopath, optimizing wellness for businesses with heart. A woman after my own heart, both in values and metaphors!

I told Meredith I thought that she presented a great foundation to build on and I was very excited to be working with her. "This is going to be great! So, where shall we start? Operations? Sales? HR?" I bubbled enthusiasm. Meredith looked at the floor.

"Well, hmm," I tried again, gentler this time, "I suppose we could start more micro and specifically look at how you would like to manage the relationship with this one new client?" Meredith shuffled her feet. The woman who had come into my office was rapidly shrinking before my eyes. Another looong minute ticked by.

"There's a lot to do, isn't there?" I noted softly. Meredith played with the button on her cuff.

"So much potential." I was speaking almost inaudibly now – almost, but not quite. She was listening. "People expect an awful lot."

Tears began to slowly trickle down Meredith's cheeks. We just sat together for ten or fifteen minutes, me doodling a little, passing a kleenex, Meredith letting her tears fall. Finally she said, "I see so clearly where this can go. I'm so lucky. This is an amazing opportunity. People I went to school with, my team from my old company – they'd give anything to do what I'm doing. My God, I'm only 30 years old and I have an assistant! Do you know how long I have wanted an assistant?! But now I have a payroll to meet. And so I landed a big account. Great! But now I have this client who is fully aware that he's the largest on my roster. He'll be calling my cell phone on Sundays soon. He knows he owns me. I pay my mother's mortgage. I take care of my brother's kid's braces. I have another proposal to do this week. It never stops. I want this, I do. So much! Yet I still don't know if I want it enough."

"Sounds more like you don't know if you want it to be *like that*. Or, really, I think you know you don't, don't you?" Meredith nodded.

"The decision is whether you can *believe* that you can let it be different, whether you can create a kind of success that you get to experience the way you want it to be," I said.

"Yes."

"How about we decide, together, right here and now, to believe that you can? That exactly that is possible. You decide what success looks like, *you* create it."

Meredith looked at me long and hard before replying, "You've really done this before? Because sometimes I feel like I'm going crazy. I should want this – it's everything I ever wanted. It's just not happening quite like

I thought it would. I mean… seriously… I mean, you've done this before? Helped people succeed even when they sometimes lose touch, sometimes don't even want to but then they do, want to, I mean, again? Oh, God, I'm not making sense. I don't even know what I mean. I guess, it's just, I mean, seriously, have you. . .?"

> **The decision is whether you can believe that you can let it be different, whether you can create a kind of success that you get to experience the way you want it to be…**

I leaned toward Meredith, put my hand on her wrist, and looked directly into her eyes before saying, "I seriously have."

Meredith held my gaze for a full thirty seconds and then said, "Let's start with operations."

Over the next year and a half, meeting weekly for three months and then on alternate weeks from there, Meredith and I spent a lot of time detailing her mission and vision for her company, building a manual of systems for client relationship management, account protocols, proposal templates. We developed a profile of her ideal client and questions she would ask herself to determine whether or not she should pursue certain projects or say yes when work was offered.

We turned that profile into an assessment tool to be administered to every client, something her assistant could also learn to do, freeing Meredith up for other things. We analyzed her sales cycle and figured out the steps she went through in the very best client relationships and developed a formula to replicate those relationships in her handling of new clients. We took apart Meredith's schedule and set "time zones" for certain types of work travel, meetings, writing, mentoring her assistant, self care, and her social life.

With each step Meredith's confidence increased. She never got over the occasional need to ask why on earth she was doing this, whether she was still on her right path – those questions don't go away, Dear Reader! Answering them just becomes matter-of-fact instead of matter-of-panic: she *did* get to a place where she knew that the impulse to ask the question stemmed from a fear of being overwhelmed, and was a valuable early warning indicator that she needed to create a bit more space for herself, schedule in some break time, reward and appreciate herself for all she was doing, refuel her energy reserves. (There is no point in being self-employed if your boss is still a slave-driver!) Helping my entrepreneur clients implement employee engagement strategies for their *own* retention is some of the most fun I ever get to have...

Two years later, Meredith had promoted her first assistant and hired two more, one full time and one part time, and she'd landed several more $5M - $10M clients. One day, when I was calling to thank her for referring a new client for me, I asked Meredith what part of our work she had found most valuable. She said her answer surprised her – but it didn't surprise me. In our third session, when she had come in with spreadsheets and marketing plans and four cross-referenced job descriptions we could use to benchmark her new assistant's role, I asked her to do a journal entry for homework for me. It's an assignment I give to most of my clients, and it never fails to work out best for those who like it the least. (Meredith, if you're wondering, *hated* it.)

Here's how we got started:

Alanna to Meredith: "Go home tonight, take a hot bath, put on your coziest clothes and make yourself whatever drink is most soothing to you..."

Meredith: "What, like wine? I shouldn't drink on a weeknight."

Alanna: "Tea. Cocoa. Wine, if it's what you find most relaxing. Hot water and lemon, whatever. Then get out your journal..."

Meredith: "I don't have a journal."

Alanna: "Stop on the way home and pick up a nice, bound notebook you can use as a journal and then take a hot bath…"

Meredith: "Then I have to stop and clean my bathtub, too."

(Some people need more help with the relaxing part of this than others, and that's okay. Nothing out of the ordinary. As it should be. I knew Meredith went someplace to get manicures and massages sometimes so I tried another tack.)

Alanna: "Okay, then, make an appointment at your favourite spa, soak in their hot tub, use their steam room, breathe in the lavender and eucalyptus and then go to their lounge area with your journal and write the following…"

Meredith: "I can't…"

Alanna: "Sure you can."

Meredith: "But…"

Alanna: "We made a deal that if you could not see how it would hurt you, in body or integrity, you'd at least *try* any suggestion I made in good faith, remember? I'm not asking you to walk the plank. It's a SPA! A little notebook & some writing! I think we both know you can handle it."

Meredith (giggling): "What do I do?"

Alanna: "Write today's date, two years from now, in the top right corner. This is your journal of the future, the future you desire, the one you are creating now. It will be a summary of all of our work together. Begin like this: 'I almost can't believe how far I've come, or how easy it all turned out to be once I let it.' And then write all the wonderful things you will have done, all the successes you will have enjoyed, all the comfort and ease you will feel, by the time we have travelled these next two years."

This conversation had to be repeated three times because weeks went by and Meredith kept not doing her homework. "I couldn't get an appointment in a spa," came the first excuse. I don't know where you live, but here in Vancouver there is a spa on just about every urban corner and a few tucked into some industrial areas as well. We are the most buffed, exfoliated, plumped and massaged generation of women – and men, in fact – that ever lived. I googled a spa directory, printed the page and told her to pick one by the following week.

And when the next week came, the excuse was: "Writing in the future is silly. It's too woo-woo. I feel goofy." Okay, you can feel goofy, no problem – it's still your homework, so you do it feeling goofy. "I don't write in journals." It's just paper and pen. Use a computer if you want – just get it done. Then came the phone calls: "Alanna, I know we're supposed to meet tomorrow but I have a deadline and I won't be able to make it…" Back and forth, excuses and drama, until, almost five weeks after we first talked about it, Meredith finally brought me a ten page journal entry, slapping the book on my desk with a "There! I hope you're happy!"

And I was.

What follows is an abbreviated but representative condensation of that journaling:

I can't believe how far I've come. When Alanna bullied me into writing this damn journal entry two years ago, I thought the whole thing was completely lame and couldn't see why or how it would do me any good.

(Nice to get the hostility out on the table right from the start, don't you think? I always tell my clients when we get going that there may be days they don't like me as much as today, and that's okay. If they like me every minute, I'm probably not doing my job to nudge them out of their comfort zones.)

I can't stand being someone who won't do her homework, though, so eventually I had to give in and do it. I wrote about how my business grew without sucking the life out of me, and how I reconnected with what I liked about my work and taking it to the next level, even though I still didn't believe I could do that. Once I got going, it turned out to be easier than I thought (she's making me say that!) Each meeting or piece of homework made a little more sense than the last, and each time I went out on a limb and did something I wasn't sure would work or didn't think I was ready for, I was pleasantly surprised.

(Meredith went about four pages like this, just working up to the idea that this journal would be an okay thing to do, 'meta-journaling' about the idea of the journal, and then eventually breaking through and beginning to write the actual contents of the journal itself.)

I started to feel more confident about my work with my new clients. I got tons of creative ideas and my work just began to flow. My assistant took on all the details and administrative stuff that can get me bogged down so I could focus on the campaign management work I really enjoy, and she took an interest in learning more about account management as well, so she could pitch in, in a meaningful way, as workload increased. Pretty soon I was earning double what I was earning the previous year, and more easily taking care of all the people in my life who need me.

I was afraid that I would be overwhelmed by all the responsibility, that I would drown in the pressure, but I eventually began to relax and know the growth would kind of take care of itself and I would have plenty of stability. I just needed to remind myself to relax into it. Cool! My second assistant came on board just 9 months after my first, like a new baby. A huge step but definitely the right one. We got slammed with a bunch of new clients just heading in the New Year and worked some crazy hours to make it all happen but it was so worth it. We pulled together as a team, figured out how to be a company and work at this level. It was trial by fire and I loved it! Good people doing a hard thing well. I forget sometimes that it's what I love but that year I remembered. By summer I was ready for a break and I took my first ever two week vacation since going out on my own> Left the whole company to C and J to run. I was so scared, but they stepped up and made it all work. They even put together a proposal for a new client and landed it all on their own!

In the second year, coming up on my fourth as a business owner, I made a commitment to running a healthy business on every level and hired a nutritionist and trainer to work with our whole team and we all ran a 10K together that Fall. We all lost the weight we gained eating donuts while writing press releases the previous winter, and felt stronger than ever. Pretty soon my life started looking so good I felt like I'd been silly to be so worried: it was really just a matter of one step at a time, focusing on the big picture, doing what works over again and refining it. I felt solid, smart and very lucky. At the end of the year, we had done record profits and I was able to offer profit-sharing to my team, do some renovations on my condo, put my 15 year-old Toyota Tercel to sleep and buy the Jeep that I've always wanted, with a roof rack for my bikes and camping gear and space in the back for friends and dogs. I love my clients and I love my life! I have come a LONG way!

I smiled as Meredith and I revisited her experience. It was now about five years after she wrote that journal, our first work term together over, followed by a three year break, then another nine months together as she tackled setting up new offices and change managing expansion to include three more people on her full time staff and a month-long trip to Southeast Asia. So what made the exercise so powerful?

"Doing it – or really not doing it for so long – made me realize how afraid I was to dream," Meredith said. "Like if I put everything I wanted down on paper, I would have to do it. It would be all about keeping up and I'd feel even more pressure. It would be even more work. But then we kept talking about my business, this homework, my life really, being my project, mine to create. Which meant I could decide to create it as doable, manageable. Hard work and long hours, yes – I don't mind that. But not drowning in pressure, all stressed out. I could feel like I was getting somewhere. And the very best part of the journaling came way later, when I would pick it up, re-read it and realize how much of that I accomplished. We did about 80% of what we set out to do in that first year and a bit alone, way more than I would have done if I hadn't trusted enough to lay it all out. Now I write a journal like that at the beginning of every year. It sets my course and keeps me there."

I have no doubt that Meredith will soon be running a major enterprise – if she chooses. She has everything she needs to make it happen.

Antonio is a client who came to me when he had about 20 people working for him, most of them subcontractors in his software development company which provided custom, web-based inventory management systems for large manufacturers, importers and exporters. I don't for a minute understand the lines of code Antonio writes or the Six Sigma-inspired warehousing and distribution systems his clients require. Fortunately, I do understand inspiring dreams, and Antonio's dream touched me deeply.

Antonio wanted to have enough growth and stability in his organization that he could turn a core team of contractors into full time salaried employees, expand sales and systems, buy a building for their offices, give shares in the company to a few key people, develop those employees into leaders over a few years, and then sell them the company in installments, working less and less himself until the company buy-out became his retirement/pension plan. Oh, is that all?!?

Antonio knew what he valued from the beginning: people, teams, quality, longevity, heart. The problem as he saw it, the gap between his considerable skills and intention and the manifestation of his dream, is that the business wasn't really scalable yet. He had over a hundred small-to-medium sized clients but what he would need to really put a foundation under the company's growth is to have three or four really big, probably multinational, corporate clients who entered into long term contracts which generated revenue every month in software customizations, training, and technical support.

Antonio was clear, confident and ready to get down to work, so we put together a plan to manage his time so he could carve out eight hours per week to work on his 'big fish' goals while maintaining his current responsibilities. We reviewed a previous year's worth of Requests-for-Proposal (RFPs) to see what his client companies were looking for, and strategized the capacity-building he would need to do to handle the workload when he big clients came on board. We evaluated the performance of all of his contractors and identified which ones seemed like the best candidates to be his first full time, permanent employees, and sought legal counsel on his corporate structure and employment agreements.

Finally, the first 'big deal' RFP was written and he made it through the screening round to have an opportunity to present his offerings in person to the management team at a large and well-known corporation. So, naturally, that's when all the resistance Antonio had ever felt about his business came pouring out to knock our carefully laid plans well off the rails!

"I can't work with people like that!" Antonio exploded as his presentation date loomed. "They're all put together. Their expectations. . . I mean. . . I can't. . . I mean. . . Well, %$#! I can never fit in, not in that world!"

Antonio was not a man given to profanity; in fact, he was circumspection itself as I knew him. I sat up a little: I knew this was going to be a good day for his business. "What world?" I asked.

"With those corporate dragons!" he blurted incredulously, like I must be terribly dense because *everyone* sees anyone with an office and a pinstripe suit somewhere in their closet as a character out of King Arthur's court or Harry Potter. I smiled. The choice of images here is actually highly instructive. The stage of work/life development at which Antonio found himself was a place I see my clients pass through often – and by that

> I've noted one, and really only one, major difference between the people who eventually break through barriers and soar to great heights and those who stay more stuck. People who go farther and live deeper have found more of a comfort level with fear, and with ambiguity.

I mean revisiting or cycling through often for each one of them, not just once each by a volume of clients. Nope, dragon-land is a regular stopping place. How long and how often we stop is all about what we do when we get there.

"Here's what I see," I said. "In fifteen years of walking alongside people while they sort out their goals and pursue different career and business paths, I've noted one, and really *only one*, major difference between the people who eventually break through barriers and soar to great heights and those who stay more stuck. People who go farther and live deeper have found more of a comfort level with fear, and with ambiguity. The people you think are more successful – and let's be clear that I don't accept the premise that simply having a corporate job or earning a certain dollar figure equates with success, even subjectively, but let's just accept, lightly, some hypothetical shared understanding of what work/life success is – those people have all the same fears and doubts and baggage as anyone else. They have just learned how to recognize fear as a frequent companion on their journey, rather than something to be rid of before they can move forward, thus they don't get stopped as often or for as long as many other people do."

"Great. So successful people like fear?" Antonio mumbled cantankerously under his breath.

"Well, yeah," I mused, noting not for the first time how few words it sometimes takes to make my point. "Successful people have learned to like fear. Some have gone so far as to make fear a best friend or close associate, understanding that excitement and challenge are often equal parts desire and fear, and it's the prospect of facing our fear that charges us as much as any other part of the experience we seek. And those other successful people, probably the lion's share of the group, while not sold on becoming bosom buddies, have at least learned to like fear enough to pass some time with it, like a co-worker or acquaintance. Fear is at least not intolerable to them."

"So the rest of us won't let fear be our friend." Yup. Antonio was really catching on. And his succinctness impressed the hell out of me.

"So how come it feels like we have to fight it?" he puzzled. I wish I had good answer for that one. Many people smarter than I have devoted their lives to cultural anthropology and similar studies to look at where human beings have filed 'fear' in their social vernacular. They haven't come to complete consensus, and I can't begin to do justice to their research. What I can say is that many societies make a dance with fear part of a rite of passage to help a young person learn how to move forward in life: think Joseph Campbell's *Hero with a Thousand Faces* or the solitary vision quests of Aboriginal peoples. And that's where Antonio's first analogy becomes so apt: the dragon. When we learn to walk with fear instead of fighting it, we move forward with a companion a little closer to Puff, the Magic Dragon, and a little less like Smaug, the fire-breathing carnivore of Tolkien legend.

Antonio had already come so much farther in his professional life than most people ever will, and he was getting ready to do something very hard, which should not be diminished. But that's what he signed up to do. Entrepreneurs are not the sort of people who can be happy playing it safe. They went out of their own to forge their own destiny for a reason. It can just be hard to remember that reason some days, and that's when it's good to have someone else around who holds that memory, holds the space where desire still lives.

I reminded Antonio of the number of clients I have who see him as a 'dragon.' People like Meredith, in fact, who couldn't even imagine managing 10 people on her team, let alone the 20 he had, let alone his grand and beautiful vision of turning his company over to his employees one day.

"Yeah," Antonio said, "But you and I know it just looks that way to her because she's not there yet. When you get here, you find it's all the same stuff, just more people."

"Exactly!" I replied. Antonio was getting better and better at making my points for me. "And here's what I know about my corporate executive clients like the ones you'll speak to next week: they can't understand why you see *them* as dragon-worthy. They know that they do the same stuff, too, just with more people and more zeroes on the invoice. And somewhere in their goals for next year is securing account with a company that they think of as so big it's become mythic to them, and they are scared to give the presentation they need to give. We all construct dragons out of our fears sometimes. That doesn't change. *We* change."

"Okay," Antonio sighed. "Uncle. I'll give the presentation." We focused on reviewing his intention for the meeting, ensuring he was not cutting any corners, that all of his methods and proposals would scale to whatever size the business might grow to and whatever a large client's needs might be. The real gift of the proposal process turned out to be the way it provoked him to look intensely at every aspect of this business: the big fish client he wanted but didn't think he was ready for provided the lens through which to evaluate all of his systems and processes, and make them better at their work for all levels of clients, and for the benefit of his team themselves. Necessity is still the mother of invention more times than not, after all.

Antonio didn't wind up getting that first big bid – another gift because he was able to lower his fears further by seeing, up close, with his own eyes, that even very large companies were sometimes constrained by budget and timeline. The principals on that bid told him they thought he had the superior product but they needed something simpler and more cost-effective just this one time. I think Antonio was happier to get that feedback complimenting and contextualizing his product in the market than he would have been to get the contract! It told him he was on the right track yet gave us a bit more time to work through his fears before he did his next RFPs – both of which he did close. For many months to come, as he began counting as clients and friends many large, corporate 'pin stripe types,' as he liked to call them, Antonio would pause and take note when fear came along to join him.

I can't say he ever got to love it, but he doesn't go to pieces, anymore: he just kind of laughs at himself, rubs his beard and gets back to work building his empire. (Oh, and a picture of Puff the Magic Dragon, torn from one of his son's pop-up books, adorns Antonio's desk to this day...)

Chapter 8

Where Everybody Knows Your Name:

Workplace Relationships for Better or for Worse

Every career – like every life, I would argue – is built in large part on relationships. We rely on classmates and friends to make it through school and our early years; we build relationships in our job interviews and leverage networks to secure those interviews and create a place for ourselves in an organization; and our experience of our careers over time is often determined more than anything else by how we feel about the people who make up our workplace community, how valued we feel by them and how connected we feel to them.

The *Cheers* song from which I have taken my title for this chapter says, "Making your way in the world today / Takes everything you've got."

If what you've got includes a good team around you, work takes a lot less out of you and gives a lot more to you; if you don't, at a certain point you are likely to decide that it's just not worth it. And sometimes, you've got to figure out how to somehow hold on to the team without forcing yourself to hang on in a job that has stopped working for you.

Knowing when and how to shore up your relationships and when and how to "break up" with one company to start fresh with another thus forms the centre of this chapter.

Sometimes in the process of turning your work upside down to get a life that reflects your authentic vision of yourself, you start to hear voices. Not in the *Sybil* or *Sixth Sense,* "I am vast, I contain multitudes of dead people" way, mind you, but in the "hmmm... I must have internalized my father/Aunt Millie/first grade teacher/last boyfriend on that one" way. We take in a lot more than we realize from the people around us, a lot of it just seeping in without notice – so much so that sometimes, despite even our very best intentions, what we are trying to do and what we actually create with our actions are worlds apart. This is perhaps nowhere more true than in the ways we approach our relationships, and just as true in work as in the rest of life.

My client, Michaela, a freshly promoted 38 year-old television producer with her first direct reports and quarterly budgets to manage, came to me for assistance when workplace politics issues were making it hard for her to love the very job she'd been working toward for well over a decade. As you might imagine, breaking into television is no small feat: like fashion, professional sports, music, perhaps travel writing and elite event planning, it's one of those professions where, as my Dad used to say, "many are called but few are chosen." It's also the kind of work which outsiders assume is all celebrity parties and awards shows, completely unaware of the many years of ego-crushing, back-breaking labour that goes into the paying of dues, and then the jolt of 'making it' only to face overwhelming time and money pressures, compounded by constant worry about losing one's place in an exceedingly competitive industry. In film and tv, many clients have told me, even off camera there can be a new flavour-of-the-month 'star' and no, you're not paranoid – some people really are out to take your job!

For those who love it, though, who come alive in the fiery mix of creativity, communication, connection and possibility, there is no option other than to pursue the dream. Michaela had been around long enough to know every inch of the downside of her chosen profession. She'd also dabbled in and out of her industry a bit in those first early years and knew there was really nothing else she'd rather do. She'd given her heart as a young girl volunteering at a small town cable station and there was no looking back. The choice, then, was one of making this work for her, of being responsible for and accountable to her own experience, knowing that she wasn't going to change an industry but she could change herself… and, if we did it right, hopefully influence some of the dynamics in the small corner that was the production team she led, as well.

Picking up that earlier thread about 'voices' in our heads, what Michaela and I realized early on is that her self talk echoed the sounds of a cacophonous band playing many confusing tunes. There were the voices of her parents who had wanted her to choose something more stable like Accounting or Law and who she could always count on to show up in her mind on a bad day with some chastising version of "We told you it would be like this" (though they had really said no such thing and had no way of knowing how "it" would be to work in broadcasting, anyway). There were the voices of the friends who thought she had it made, many of whom were admiring and supportive, but a few who were envious and responded to her successes with "Gee, must be nice" jabs and a hint of a smile when small things went wrong.

Then there were those who thought she had it made and were outright jealous of her, passive aggressively arguing that she worked too hard, the hours were impossible, why was she doing that to herself, she should get a real job, playing at that tv station for so little money and recognition was crazy, boy I'm glad my job isn't like that! (Sabotage disguised as support can be very hard to diagnose, let alone cope with.) It was the actual voices at the station, though, and one from her past it took us awhile to identify, which were having the greatest impact on Michaela's experience of her work.

Michaela's workplace was full of shop talk, cross talk and behind-the-back talk. People can work some quite literally *insane* hours in television to meet broadcast deadlines. I had one client a number of years ago who called me after she had worked 50 hours straight – not in a week, mind you, in a *row*! No sleep, not even leaving the building or changing clothes – this on a mix of coffee and donuts, pizza and pepsi, a staple diet chased down with chocolate-covered espresso beans, all to get last-minute reshoots and edits to air... I was surprised she was still breathing, let alone talking to me!

Where live programming is being shot, the adrenaline is not unlike an operating room or rescue operation, but with less of the countervailing calm. In any organization like this, certainly not exclusive to tv or film, the culture can become its own little world, a veritable 'Young and Restless' of gossip. Everyone has an opinion on everything, with sleep deprivation and stress contributing to a disproportionate number of negative opinions in that mix.

Michaela contacted me after the fourth or fifth planning meeting in which she had been sandbagged by a colleague from the station's old guard. In one meeting their management team would have a discussion about some project, policy or initiative, divvy up action items, and come back to the following meeting with each producer/manager ready to present a progress report or proposal for next steps. Occasionally this involved some footage or multi-media, but generally it was just a one page memo or talking points, usually distributed right in the moment, plus the dialogue itself.

Each time Michaela came back with her ideas, this same person, Joe, would have a go at her, point by point, objection after objection, following his remarks with thinly veiled putdowns ("Of course being so new here you couldn't possibly have known X so it is not your fault"), reminding anyone who would listen that he was the institutional memory, the experienced hand. Post-meeting, Michaela faced the pitying looks and darting glances of colleagues, and she was quite convinced she was an unflattering subject of conversation when she was not in the room. Not surprisingly, she hated it.

Michaela had run many projects over her career, spearheading production on particular segments or shows, but this was her first time in an institutional management role, with a set staff reporting to her year-round, not just contracted for the piece, and with long term budgets, resource allocation, operations and systems to worry about. From her description of events, it was clear that both her discomfort with her new responsibility and her considerable strategic talent were showing – and Joe, one of her more senior peers in the organization, was using her vulnerability to score points and maintain his place in the pecking order. He was old school: best defense is a good offense. Sure, if you want your life to be a war. I certainly don't. And happily Michaela didn't either.

I asked Michaela what she felt as she prepared for and walked into these meetings.

"Sick to my stomach, frankly," came her rueful reply. "I am great at pointing a camera, figuring out what to shoot, getting people to open up, telling the story. I'm even pretty good in the edit suite and not bad at marketing. But that's all art, really. Communication, being creative. I'm not built for business. I don't know if taking this promotion was the right move."

"*I'm not built for business?*" I queried. "That's a pretty sweeping statement for a woman who has made a good living in show business for, what has it been, thirteen years? You don't work in some experimental artists' colony – you've always worked in business. Maybe not directly with the spreadsheets and governance as much as now, but you've always scoped and costed projects. Where's that voice coming from?"

"I don't know. I've just always believed it. I hate math, hate worrying about money. And I hate these business-driven management meetings where everyone is jockeying for position," Michaela fumed.

"Hate 'em enough to give up producing or hate 'em enough to change how you look at them once and for all?" I asked.

"That's a crappy choice!" Michaela objected.

"I admit there are variations on the options that we can and will explore, but you and I both know they will tend to be flavours of 'Take *on* the challenge of changing your beliefs and fears so you can stay in a healthy way' or 'Take *off* – change employers or even industries.' There is a lot of middle ground but it's still divided on one side or another of that line. So what's it gonna be?"

"Fight or flight, huh?" Michaela asked.

"No – no fighting. I admit I used to believe in that, mostly because it's what I knew how to do. Maslow says when all you have is a hammer, you tend to see a lot of nails! I have many more tools than that in recent years and I rarely advise a fight anymore. I'm thinking more along the lines of getting very conscious of your own power and intentions and then more like absorbing your opponent's power to flow with your own – think of it as martial arts rather than boxing. Care to try?" I invited as Michaela hesitantly nodded.

"Okay, the first thing I would suggest is for you to start reading some biographies of business people you admire and bestsellers on anything about leadership – any type of business is fine. I just want you to get used to the vocabulary, immerse yourself a little, see it's not so foreign, and, I'm betting, realize that successful businesspeople start from all sorts of different places and you know more than you think."

"You know," Michaela said, "I can maybe even do one better. One of the shows in my department is doing a couple of features on some national business leaders. I'm the one who decides who works on which project..."

"I like where your mind is going!" I said. "Why read biographies when you can create them? Perfect! My other piece of homework is for you to start shoring up some relationships around your department. You're new; no one knows you. When they *do* know you and you know them, it will be easier to feel like you hold your own space in the meetings and harder for someone like Joe to make his projection of you more meaningful to other colleagues than their own experience of you. That may be the easiest assignment I ever give you!"

"Okay, but let's take care not to turn me into some kissass suck-up," Michaela pled under her breath.

"I'm sorry – what did you just say?" I asked, reasonably sure I heard but definitely needing to check in.

"I'll get to know some of the other exec producers a little if you think it's best, but I hate people who are always trying to get everyone to like them, chameleons, playing politics, all obsequious and sycophantic. That's no better than Joe and I'm not going to do that," Michaela spouted.

"There's a lot of energy behind that viewpoint," I observed. "Almost more force than I've heard you speak about anything. What does that mean to you?"

"You know what I mean," she said, irritated.

"I don't know if I do or not. Humour me. Explain," I replied.

"I don't want to be the 'let's do lunch' girl who can't get by on her ideas or the quality of her work so has to kiss a bunch of asses to get ahead," Michaela declared.

This is a viewpoint I hear a lot, to varying degrees. People who don't like or have been burned by workplace politics – usually because they tried to pretend there were no politics – now want to believe that all politics are all bad. I tend to think that 'politics' is just a negative way of saying the way relationships are approached, and once we shift the vocabulary to

> ...Politics – usually because they tried to pretend there were no politics – now want to believe that all politics are all bad. I tend to think that 'politics' is just a negative way of saying the way relationships are approached, and once we shift the vocabulary to something at least neutral and possibly even positive, we can start shifting the paradigm.

something at least neutral and possibly even positive, we can start shifting the paradigm as well.

"What makes you assume that merely having workplace relationships is tantamount to covering up for some inadequacies, Michaela? Why can't you be well known, well liked and also well qualified?" I challenged.

"I dunno," came her reply, the voice a little different than the triple word score which had argued before. I tried a couple more ways to draw out an answer but Michaela was feeling stuck that day so it seemed like it was time for a change of subject. I just planted the seed that the source of her beliefs and perhaps also a shift in them would come to her over the coming weeks if she remained open to it, and instead revisited the idea of some intra-company networking.

"I don't want you to falsely compliment anyone or pitch yourself or 'try' in any way to gain favour. I just want you to pick two people per week in your management meetings and invite them for coffee or lunch and then have whatever conversation comes up. Don't let them go to gossip or manipulation, either, of course: you've been interviewing for long enough to know how to gracefully get into or out of a subject area if you want to. This is just getting to know one another, plain and simple," I argued.

"Sounds manipulative to me. How can it be 'just' getting to know one another when you are only telling me to do it because of Joe?" Michaela argued back.

"I'd have to say that's faulty causation, Miss Rhetorician," I laughed. "I learned that you had not built relationships on your team during a conversation about both Joe and about your discomfort in your new role; that doesn't make Joe the cause of my sentiment on this. No matter how I found out about it, once I learned you were not making friends and influencing people, I would have made this suggestion eventually. Count on it. This is Career Strategy 101."

"But I don't want people to think I am sucking up to them!" Michaela burst out.

This was one of those funny times in life when we learn about self perception. On any given spectrum of characteristics (greedy to generous; gregarious to shy; intransigent to acquiescent), particularly when our motivation is aversion of one pole rather than attraction to its opposite, we very often have a skewed perception of what we are putting out there. I grew up in a very demonstrative household, for example: big talk, big hugs, big drama, and huuuge meals. When one of my guest's adamant refusal of a third or fourth helping (despite my mother's starting to actually put the food on his plate!) sparked laughter around the table, my Dad interjected, "Come now, can't have people thinking we starve our guests." If you're worried about not starving people, it's quite possible you'll fail to notice you are actually stuffing them – or, as my boyfriend at the time observed later that evening, "raising generosity to an act of aggression."

Michaela was so worried about not being manipulative or using gamesmanship to cover up incompetence, she was unable to see that she was actually being a little cold – some break time or après work socializing is fairly typical professional behaviour, after all. She also failed to realize that she had her head down so much and focused so intently on her production team, no one would ever think she was incompetent as a producer. If she didn't build some relationships in management soon, though, people *would* begin to see her as incompetent as a leader, and I gently told her so.

Michaela grudgingly agreed to try to fit in two social interactions at work the following week and, to her conscientious credit, had kept her word when she next came to see me. She was not, however, in any way happy about it. "People were looking at us. Joe was looking at us. I know they were wondering what we were doing, and I hate being gossiped about!" she said.

"People were wondering about your walking across the street from the studio to grab a Starbucks?" I asked. "Don't you do that, like, every couple of minutes around there?"

"Yes but not with anyone else!" she said, like I had lost a few dozen IQ points since our last meeting.

"Michaela, I need you to listen to yourself for a minute," I said. "On this one subject you do not sound in any way like the woman I know. There is no reasoning with you. And, frankly, there is also no reason coming out of you, either. Over the past few weeks I've grown to like and care about this passionate, insightful, principled woman who wants to change the world with great programming that reaches the widest possible audience – and then it's like 'Elvis has left the building' when I ask about workplace relationships. Michaela who? Suddenly I'm here with 'fear of coffee date' woman. Who are you and what have you done with my client?"

Michaela progressed from grinning to laughing out loud. Good. I needed her to be a little more relaxed for this. "I think we really need to take a look at what's going on because this looks to me like the kind of thing that is going to keep getting in your way."

"Actually, um, I think I know what it is," Michaela said softly. I waited. "My grandfather. He lived with us when I was small. He always told me to be independent, don't be a fish, don't take the bait, never let them suck you in. I guess he went off with the in-crowd when he was young and didn't finish school or something and it was important to him that I be super professional, work hard, not get distracted."

"Did he have a few ideas about authenticity, too, I'm guessing?" I asked.

"He never liked my sister – always thought she 'played false' as he called it, pretended to care about him when she needed something and was never around otherwise. He made me promise I would never be like her," she said tearfully. "And I never have."

"And you never have. I know."

> **If these tactics worked...I needed to know. Because that's not a battle worth fighting, even if I could have won it. That's a phone ringing with a message saying my next life was calling.**

"But I can also see how I maybe get mixed up sometimes. There is a difference between using people and having friends you can ask for things." Michaela paused for a minute, like she was hearing what she had just said for the first time, then added, "And I think I can trust myself to know the difference." I told her I thought so, too.

Coffee and lunch dates got to be the norm for Michaela, and so did bouncing big picture ideas around outside of meetings, just in the hallway or on set. She learned how to pitch a budget idea to one of her peers the same way she could pitch a story idea to a prospective interview. She even took one friendship all the way out of the office to a concert one night, and we laughed as she reflected back on how far she had come that something so ordinary had once seemed so impossible.

Dealing with Joe hadn't gotten that much easier, though. Michaela was realizing that she knew a lot more about business than she had been giving herself credit for, but she was still intimidated by Joe's hostility toward her, and let him get the better of her in several more meetings. I was concerned that the more energy we gave to worrying about Joe, the more power we were giving him over her. While I wanted to support her to change the dynamic between them, I wanted to do that by changing how Michaela perceived her own power, not by letting Joe become the point of our work.

"But he makes me look foolish! He is positively Machiavellian!" Michaela exclaimed.

I'm no stranger to Machiavellian tactics. I once had a new colleague in an organization befriend me, lots of one-on-one talks, exchanges of ideas, lunches here and there, always getting around in some way to exploration of philosophies that "we" shared and ideas that "we" would someday advance to upper management, all warm and fuzzy. When a few months later I went on holiday, he delivered a 17 point memo to our senior, outlining his personal plan for organizational and brand turnaround... 14 of those points straight out of my mouth... though (oops!) somehow without attribution. Must've slipped his mind. He had several business days while I was away to flesh out 'his' ideas, give his rationale, coax buy-in and take bits of brainstorming to their next iteration. By the time I walked back into it, he was the de facto owner of what felt like every suggestion I had ever made.

I had to give him credit. His strategy was brilliant: there was absolutely no way I could take the position that any part of the plan was mine without looking like a spoiled child. So instead I kept my mouth shut, publicly thanked him for his synthesis, and silently thanked him for giving me a new barometer with which to evaluate my organization. If these tactics worked, if my manager would buy that this detailed analysis came out of the new guy's first exposure to systems and policies, and if he would allow his memory to be blighted to where many of those very familiar ideas had originated and first been expressed to him, this was good information for me. I needed to know. Because that's not a battle worth fighting, even if I could have won it. That's a phone ringing with a message saying my next life was calling.

On this day, I was also thankful because the experience had given me very good insight on how to help clients like Michaela: having been cornered into silence myself, I know how it worked; having risen above such tactics to create a much better future than my present in that moment, I also knew how to support Michaela so she did not have to stoop anywhere close to that level.

Our master plan for Michaela went like this: She would set the intention that everyone had her best interests and the best interests of the station in mind and treat them accordingly. She'd interact with and respond to every person, including Joe, like they were smart, positive and helpful. That would include building relationships throughout and beyond her division, openly and thoughtfully – not because she was planning to make some power play, but because this was her community, made up of people we just decided were smart, positive and helpful, remember? It would also include doing her level best to present the best possible ideas and deliver quality work – no problem there.

It might also include, though, running through ideas before a key meeting to get some feedback and clarity: this a key behaviour she had been avoiding in a mistaken belief that it would make her look inexperienced or disingenuous. When you choose to believe your team is on your side, you naturally find transparent communication and asking for help a little easier, which would pretty organically have the net effect of making them more likely to be on your side, of course!

It finally also meant taking a detached and compassionate look at Joe: he was 58 to her 38, facing sweeping changes in technology and culture that he never could have foreseen when he got into the business, and then the faces in his world kept changing, too. Sometimes a good friend was replaced by a spiffy up-and-comer who would scare him for awhile. Through that lens Joe looked vulnerable, not intimidating, and Michaela could step back into her power and address some of Joe's likely needs at the same time: no sacrifice or compromise. Win/win.

Does this spiritually-minded path sound a little too hearts and flowers to some of you? I can understand that. I would once have said so myself. Then I did a few informal return on time and energy investment studies in my own life and came to see that this path was a shortcut – and a very strategic one at that. The 'tactical' version of the same moves would involve

Michaela 'positioning' herself as knowledgeable, beefing up relationships with strategically identified allies while doing what she could to neutralize Joe. She'd also be well advised to have a 'pre-meeting' or two before the main meeting, stopping by Joe's desk and dropping hints about a few of her weaker ideas, letting him put on the Edward De Bono black hat of which he seemed to be so fond where she is concerned and shoot down her thoughts at will – in private rather than public.

Michaela would then be in a position to go into the management meeting and thank Joe for his help in shaping her thinking – couldn't have done it without him – and deliver her ideas in a way that, having given him half the credit, he can't really attack her anymore. As far as every person in the room is concerned, Joe is now on Michaela's side and he would have to be willing to be a complete jerk to step up and say, "Well, thanks Michaela, for so generously complimenting and validating me, but I still think you are wrong-headed..." I'd say there are overwhelming odds against him making that choice, and zero odds that anyone would take his side over hers if he did: Joe would look way too petty to win allies with this kind of behaviour.

The tactical approach would work in most cases, I'm sure. But it would be exhausting and joyless. It would also need constant monitoring and repeating. And the same tactics could only work once or twice: Joe is going to catch on, feel like he has been played – because he has! – and he's going to shift tactics. No matter how cleanly Michaela is able to play the game, she is nonetheless still playing a game. To be clear, I should say that I don't have an ethical problem with the tactics described here; rather I think they are pretty positive as tactics go, and I am open to the idea that there may be times in your life when you may genuinely be facing a nail and you therefore really need a hammer.

I just don't think tactics go as far as heart can go. Ever. And that belief is all about results. While the first tactical win might feel good, the need to fight another round is going to wear very thin. These kinds of absurd battles of attrition are precisely how workplaces become toxic and employee assistance programmers who provide stress counselling start singing "ka ching!"

The alternative is so simple as to be almost absurd to need pointing out. *Actually* choosing to like people. Actually treating them with respect.

Actually being transparent. Coming from a belief that all of us can influence our experience of our lives with our choices. Maslow again! Higher human values and self-actualization. No monitoring. No maneuvering. Michaela and I decided she would succeed in just being real – with herself, her colleagues, even with Joe. Ask for input; benefit from the team; and then thank them for real. And if somebody still on occasion behaves badly and body checks someone else in a planning meeting? Talk about that for real, too. These practices feel a whole lot better than tactics, and in my experience they work more efficiently and effectively, too. When we come from love and decide to look for love, it's pretty hard to find much else.

Okay, so the next logical question is: what if, try as you might, when you look inside yourself in the context of where you work, you honestly can't find real respect, real fondness or real communication? Or despite your very best efforts, it turns out this organization is too far gone for anyone to reciprocate the respect you are giving them? That's that phone ringing again – new employer on line two. Your tactics don't change: leaving will be the most loving thing you do for yourself and for them.

And the question after that? What happens when the situation is reversed? When the love is for the people and the problem is the job or the culture? Loyalty to our fellows can get us to do just about anything – it's what the military relies on to get soldiers to fight a war so you can certainly expect it could keep us in line in some insurance agency or manufacturing company!

It's a lot easier to decide whether to stay or go in a job when the decision-making criteria are cut-and-dried, easily measurable. When the variables are layered, messy, and shifting around the edges instead of neatly pulling into sharp focus, life can feel pretty complicated and we can easily feel paralyzed. Einstein is often quoted as saying that "Not everything that can be counted actually counts, and not everything that counts can be counted." And we sometimes can't see either clearly.

It would not be too hard to decide to leave a job you have only been in for two months where you are commuting three hours per day to an airless office where you are spoken to by none of your co-workers, disrespected by your boss 100% of the times she speaks to you and paid $25,000 per year less than standard market rate for your industry and level of responsibility. Clearly, the numbers just don't add up in a whole bunch of areas that count.

But what about when you have been happy in a place for a number of years and your satisfaction is slowly eroding in ways it is hard to diagnose? Or you know you are making less than some of your friends, but it is enough to maintain your lifestyle and, gee, you think the company probably can't

> I just don't think tactics go as far as heart can go. Ever. And that belief is all about results. While the first tactical win might feel good, the need to fight another round is going to wear very thin.

afford more, and you don't want to be greedy? Perhaps you have dozens of friendly relationships with your co-workers — no one super special to whom you owe great loyalty but no one that you can strongly object to, either? Or you know enough about what a lot of other people do to know that you are really very lucky by comparison, and you have a vague sense that maybe it just doesn't get better than this and you should focus on being grateful instead of looking for greener pastures on the other side of a fence you can't really see in your mind's eye, anyway?

Whew! These are tough choices. It's like the famous science experiment with the frog: throw him into boiling water and he reacts immediately to save himself, bottoming and jumping out. Put him into tepid water and just slowly turn up the heat and he swims around unaware of the danger until he loses consciousness and is boiled alive. I usually prefer the jolt of boiling water for my clients; when it's not there, I try to provide a splash of cold because there are way more of us living over a hot burner than we realize. That cold water usually takes the form of finding creative and deeply personal ways to select and then count what needs to be counted in order to make conscious career choices.

Jeffrey Hollender, CEO of the widely respected green products firm, Seventh Generation (coming from the Iroquois First Nation's practice of considering the impact of any decision on the next seven generations, the company name says a great deal about how Hollender runs his organization), in his brilliant book on values-based business called *What Matters Most,* demands that we learn to measure the hitherto unmeasurable. Doing what real leaders do and saying not "Hey, follow me!" but rather "Okay, I'll go first," Hollender tells us this about Seventh Generation:

> In our business, we have gone to what some might regard as inordinate lengths to answer such imponderable questions as, "How can you measure how passionate people are or how safe they feel about walking into the CEO's office and saying what's really on their mind?" We've come to consider the company as a place in which to offer people an opportunity not just for material and economic growth, but spiritual and moral and personal growth as well. We've tried to create a corporate culture in which people are not drained by their work but energized by it, not alienated but fulfilled as members of an intentional community. (p. x)

With these questions which inform the discussion throughout this important book, Hollender offers a great summary of the questions I invite my clients to answer for themselves. If your employer is not providing this holistic growth opportunity and intentional community, it's time to look elsewhere. Not "time in your life" – I understand we haven't met so I wouldn't presume to say that to you! Rather I mean time in history, time in the evolution of how we look at work and life, who we are, why we are here and how we want to live. Hollender is just one of a large choir of voices singing a new song of inclusion, possibility and social responsibility. And if my call sheet is any indication, companies are listening! There has never been a better time to renegotiate your relationship with your work – not just your job, mind you, but your beliefs about, expectations of, and contributions to work. To enjoy an intentional community, you have to be prepared to live an intentional life. To know great love in your work, you must be willing to create and share love.

So what if you are the person with all the unmentionably hard-to-measure measurables? No clear cut lines? I confess that was me not all that long ago, at least in part, so don't think for a minute that I don't feel compassion for the conundrum. But as my twice-born friends from the "Blessings in Disguise" world know (see Chapter 9), conundrums can also be great sources of joy when we find our way through them.

I was self employed in private practice for a number of years when I was offered several interesting contracts in a row – all of them possible to do in addition to my practice, some long hours for a short time, yet worth it for not just the revenue but the exposure to new organizational cultures, new sectors and ideas, and some good old fashioned professional stretching. And then I was offered a chance to help start up a multidisciplinary firm, developing a comprehensive coaching program and a team that would deliver it, with a potential depth of resources that was very exciting to me.

So off I went with a very grand vision and a huge desire to build something big from the ground up. Like Emily Dickinson, as I have noted elsewhere, "I dwell in Possibility," and I was carried away by the dream. And the dream carried me for the first year – challenge, adventure, new horizons, lots of growth. I hired or helped to hire six or seven new people I respected and grew to care about. In the second year our core team again doubled and pressures to keep up with that level of growth began mounting. It gradually became clear for me that my vision, both for the company and for what I wanted to do with my life, was different than my CEO's and that I did not have the power to implement my vision in that environment. Yet I was so invested in what I had built within the company, I took such deep ownership of my work, and I still had such earnest hopes for what it *could* be, I couldn't see my way clear to walk away from it.

I knew I wasn't in a healthy place for me, wasn't able to grow where I so wanted and needed to grow – but where I had grown was in great fondness for my clients and my staff and that was tearing me up inside. I knew that the very distorted version of life/work balance I was living and the often wrenching conflicts about mission, direction and tactics were draining my energy and making it harder for me to do my work well. Looking back, it's easy to see that it was a frog-like slow boil, but I didn't know it then. Whatever disagreements I may have felt in principle, I was confident I was nonetheless helping people, standing in good service, and thus I somehow felt I owed it to both clients and staff to be 'loyal' and fight the good fight. My personal failure was in hiding from myself for a time a truth I had long known: a 'good fight' is an oxymoron. Where the desired end is peace and love, there can be no other path.

Clarity came in the realization that if any client described experiencing their workplace culture as negatively as I was experiencing mine, I would tell them to leave. Unequivocally. And as soon as possible. And I have never asked a client to do something I was unprepared to do. That realization put my integrity on the line and demanded a response.

In the end – or, more to the point, the new beginning – gratitude is what got me through. Finding a way to be thankful for what I had learned, thankful for being someone who will take risks and build, and thankful that I was ready to stand in what I knew and do it differently going forward, shed a very energizing and clarifying light. Once I got there, I really didn't have to do anything else. I set the intention that I would leave as soon as I could prepare a thoughtful exit strategy. Literally within days, before I could do any planning let alone move to action, the universe offered up a big neon Exit sign for me, pointing to a path lined with ease and grace and a beautiful stepping into myself which has grown in empowerment and joy every day since.

And the relationships which I felt somehow 'obligated' me to stay in a place that was no longer right for me? Some survived; some deepened; others fell away without notice. As it should be, had to be. Staying past what was healthy for me was never about the relationships, anyway: that was just a story I told myself to rationalize the fear, reminding me now that no matter how much we know we know better, we don't know better every day. We all have our moments when we need another viewpoint, a higher vantage – and a lot of compassion.

I wish for every reader of this book – indeed for every person who *works* – a workplace community that is intentional, vibrant, equally challenging and supportive, where the aspects of work which deepen our humanity are counted and made to count… and where lots of people know your name!

Chapter 9

Blessings in Disguise:

Stories of Career Death and Rebirth

Elizabeth Lesser's brilliant book, *Broken Open,* a meditation on the subject of blessings in disguise in all aspects of life, begins like this:

> How strange that the nature of life is change, yet the nature of human beings is to resist change. And how ironic that the difficult times we fear might ruin us are the very ones that can break us open and help us blossom into who we were meant to be.

Later, she recounts dozens of heartfelt stories of the 'twice-born' – people who faced crisis as a catalyst, stayed awake for the process, and began anew. Lesser quotes a poem by Bunan, a Japanese Zen Master, who, in this message at once evoking the graceful syntax of Rumi and the elegant brevity of skateboarder vernacular, entreats us all:

> Die while you are alive
> and be absolutely dead.
> Then do whatever you want:
> It's all good.

For the clients whose blessings in disguise fill these pages, and indeed for this writer, dying while alive has brought beautiful rebirth.

Does it seem dramatic to refer to career change, even a career catastrophe, as a death? Think about it a little longer. What's the first question you typically ask of someone after their name? "Ah, nice to meet you. And what do you do?" And what is the reason we ask those questions? I would hope it is in part because we have an awareness that what we do can be a very deep and intimate sharing, a reflection of who we really are, of what and how we love. As an extension of that in our society, our jobs very often shape our primary sense of identity. Whether or not you find this congruent with your values or might prefer another etymology of self, it is news to no one that in western culture we tend to think of who we *are* as what we *do*. And so to lose that doing can feel like losing our being as well.

The loss of a job or career path is only one of many major life events which cause us to lose our sense of self – it strips away the comfortable identity we use to get us through the day. What probably springs to mind as I say that is the prospect of someone trapped in half a life, wearing mask to work each day and pretending to be someone they are not or even pretending to know who they are when they don't, and certainly that is sometimes the case. But the workaday 'twice born' can just as easily lose an identity that was authentically and beautifully who they were happy to be… only the world changed so much that they couldn't be that person in the same way anymore.

I've mourned and healed with clients as they faced career deaths that were painful, wrenching, grief-stricken... and also transforming, epiphanic, and to-a-person perceived to be the best thing that ever happened to them. These are some of their stories.

> **I've mourned and healed with clients as they faced career deaths that were painful, wrenching, grief-stricken... and also transforming, epiphanic, and to-a-person perceived to be the best thing that ever happened to them.**

When I met Maureen, I was immediately drawn to her composure and inner knowing – remarkable in a 27 year-old working in her first 'career' level job. She hired me because, after three years in a junior branding role for a major clothing manufacturer, she was bored and feeling stuck and had enough experience of what work could feel like, even at so young an age (or perhaps some of you might say, *especially* at so young an age, Generations Y and Z taking work/life satisfaction more for granted than their predecessors did) to know that she was not going to settle for less than her potential.

"The company is so scattered right now: expanding and contracting at the same time: one division doubling and another had some layoffs last quarter. Nobody feels like they know what they are doing. And my boss is so stressed out and lacking direction, she micromanages everything. She can't give you anything to do because she doesn't even know what it will be. And she doesn't trust anyone to initiate or finish anything because she keeps saying it's easier to do things herself than to get us up to speed. Up to speed on what, I want to know?! So I spend my days doing brand benchmarking research that she doesn't care about and writing copy that she doesn't use and surfing the net when she is not looking to see who else might be hiring. I'm a creative person and I will die if I have to stay in this job," Maureen vented quickly after we began.

And I believed her. For someone else, that might be a metaphor. But I see too often what soul-killing under-stimulation can do to a person, and a long, slow death from snuffing passion – or, worse, failing ever to ignite it – is all too common. This bright light deserved to shine, so I was very happy to get down to work and watch her start to reconnect with her brighter self.

Each meeting working on her values and goals brought new excitement and insight: Maureen took to emailing me a couple of times each day as she gave a little more thought to what she might like to do or recalled another story of a job well done. It was a joy to bask in her self-discovery every step of the way. Writing her achievements just got better as she came to see how even comparatively simple project work had quantifiable value to her company and its customers, and employed a synthesis of skills for which she had not been giving herself credit.

"People are amazing!" Maureen began on this day. "I'm completely psyched! The only challenge is going to be fitting in all these meetings around my 9-to-5 job. I am having such a good time, learning TONS!" she laughed. "I have to admit when you talked to me about this whole networking, referral meeting, leveraging relationships thing, I didn't have a whole lot of faith. I figured I would just go through the motions for a couple of weeks and then we'd try it another way."

"Humouring me is how a lot of clients get past their stopping places," I said. "I've used the metaphor of midwifery to describe being present while people give birth to themselves, but this part is almost more like a kind of surrogacy, in a way. I hold the faith you don't have yet, I carry it, and you choose to engage with yourself..."

"Through my relationship with *you*! Yes, that's exactly it," said Maureen. "I do for you what I won't do if only for myself..."

"Yes," I finished up, "and then you get to keep it, take it with you."

"So cool," came Maureen's reply. So cool, indeed, I thought. I also noted to myself that we hadn't actually talked about Maureen's current job or the career path she wanted for at least a couple of weeks, making me think she was emotionally disengaging from what we thought we were doing, which probably meant she was getting ready to open to something else.

"Pink slipped! That's what they always call it in American movies, isn't it? But no slips and no pink. Just a dumb off-white letter saying (with two spelling mistakes, thank you very much!) that my services would regrettably no longer be required. And a security guy waiting with a box for me to pack up and go. That was way too Hollywood for me. If I'd been Tom Cruise I'd have taken the whole fish tank!"

I smiled. *Jerry Maguire* is one of my favourite movies – mission statements, business start-up, optimism as a revolutionary act, you had me at hello – right up my alley. "Cameron Crowe is a genius," I responded. "But you don't need to take anyone's fish; you already know how to catch your own."

"What are you talking about?" Maureen retorted. "Everything is a mess! I was counting on that paycheque to – to –" And then the tears came. As they should, as they needed to. Flushing, clearing, creating space. We didn't do any more 'work' that day. Just hung out and sniffled. Maureen wanted an assignment when she left but I told her she would know what to do if she gave herself space to keep knowing, and she could call me when she was ready.

I've seen this happen so many times it no longer surprises me – sometimes I can even predict it, though since I could be wrong I would never say out loud before the fact. Clients come to me because they can smell that a boom is about to be lowered on their life. Suddenly a job starts feeling all wrong; their emotions are feeling very tumultuous – or flat, depending on where they started from and what it would take to push them outside their comfort zone. They can't articulate why but they have a profound knowing that they need to make a change *right now*.

They reorganize schedules, commitments, and finances to start this work as soon as possible and they jump in with both feet. Their 'spidey sense' is up, awareness heightened, yet at a completely unconscious level. They come to me for personal growth, a tweak here and tweak there, "...just a couple sessions if you can do that – don't need much," or a total overhaul, "I don't know who I am anymore and I think we'd better find out," either pole or the space between a kind of life purpose nesting instinct, lining their homes for the winter to come.

And it always happens around about the same time: we have completed all the values exploration and goal-setting; done the journaling, vision board, guided imagery of a desired future; developed a strategic plan and a time map; built a resume or business plan; researched their new market; and just started relationship building, moving them into a new community and over what is usually the most scary threshold... and then... Bankruptcy. Downsizing. Market crash. Merger or Acquisition. Lawsuit. Constructive Dismissal. Restructuring. Forced Retirement/Buyout. Sometimes even divorce, death, or diagnosis. Or several of the above.

I knew that by virtue of the knowing which had brought her to me and the vulnerability with which she had engaged in the process so far, Maureen was very well equipped to find her blessings with as much ease as anyone with whom I had ever worked. And by the time she was before me again, two days later, she was beginning to know it, too. "I've been thinking," she began. "It's kind of a good thing to have this time to really focus on myself and what I want. I can afford to take this space, not feel conflicted between their priorities and mine. I'll probably even look better to employers if I'm rested, not stressed and wound up. It's perfect timing, really – it's not like I wanted to be there, anymore. They gave me eight weeks' severance, plus my banked vacation, and some funds for outplacement. And so I was wondering..." she looked at me hopefully.

"Yes," I said. "If you can get them to reallocate the outplacement funds to me instead of to whatever firm they have chosen, I can return your remaining payments to you and that will give you a bit more of a cushion."

"Exactly!"

"Perfect!"

And yet the ride naturally still had some waves. Though she was genuinely grateful to have the space and time to do what she wanted to do, and was not sorry to have stopped filling her days with what she experienced as essentially pointless and undervalued work, Maureen was also confronting the loss of identity which came with transitional unemployment. Bad job though it had eroded into for her, it looked like a good job on the surface. It gave her emotional cover in a world where we are judged by the status

> Clients come to me because they can smell that a boom is about to be lowered on their life...They can't articulate why but they have a profound knowing that they need to make a change *right now*.

ascribed to our job titles. She had been the only one of her friends who had landed career-level employment with a major brand, earning what she called 'grown-up dollars,' enjoying a measure of self-made standing and financial security for the first time in her life, her family so proud of her, and it was hard for her at times not to experience her circumstance as both a loss and a failure.

We talked these emotions through, and I encouraged her to separate common – perhaps even inevitable – feelings of disorientation and sadness from any sense of fault, blame or diminished self worth. Most days she could do that, and some days not at all. Some days she emailed saying she had been crying for hours with no apparent trigger or cause, harder than she had cried when a good friend died, more pain than in recovery from a major surgery a few years ago, like all the grief and pain she had ever felt in her life was coming up now. I told her it *was* – that's what happens to people sometimes. It feels like it will never end, but it will. I couldn't promise her how long it would take, but I could say for certain that she wouldn't always feel this way if she hung on. I also told her that the day would come she would feel grateful for all of this, and the sooner she could feel gratitude for even small parts of it, the sooner that full healing day would come, and I know she took that in.

Yet, later, on what seemed like a better day at the start, we were working through several dry-runs of job interviews, honing her answers to over a hundred tough interview questions, the effects of her shakened centre were very evident.

"I feel like a fraud saying that I built the brand or increased sales or even managed a good campaign," she revealed. "The company is going under, more layoffs last week. My friends can't even look me in the eye anymore. And that's the ones who still return my calls – half of them don't. It's like I have some failure plague or something. My parents are all tense and sad every time I talk to them," she blurted.

"Lots of people are still working there – I'm the one who got fired in the first wave," she continued. "There's got to be a reason for that. I'm obviously not as good as I thought I was. Maybe they were just waiting for a way to get rid of me. I'm starting to think that my boss didn't give me very much to do because she didn't trust me. There's no point in going to this interview – I can't do that job. I'm not ready. I think maybe I should look for some assistant roles, maybe a coordinator. But Project Manager is too much. Not right now. Not today, anyway."

"That's the first thing you've said I'll buy," I replied. Maureen's eyes widened, blinking rapidly. "You're not feeling ready *today*. Okay, I get that. But there was a time when you did feel ready, when you were ready, and you were doing your job and doing it well for several years – during which time you had many good and even great days and lots of achievements and deep experiences of putting your talents out there and feeling what it feels like to have your amazing insides show up on the outside. You've been there before and we can go there again. Maybe not today, but conveniently your interview isn't until next week. Maybe you'll feel ready by then, maybe it will take a little while longer, maybe you won't even want this job when that day comes. But you *do* know who you are and you know you can demonstrate who you are. And I know that for you, too, even today. Especially today."

We hung out for another half hour or so, talking about some of those better days, Maureen's voice getting a little less shaky along the way. We talked about friends pulling back at a time like this, not because they are judging or abandoning her, but because they feel inadequate and don't know what to say, or because in her experience they see mirrored their own fears and vulnerabilities, and they don't want to have to look at that. Some would find a way to return to her and others would not. These are crucible experiences in life: what is true transforms into something more real; what is not true burns away.

Maureen resumed her networking and had several interviews over the next six weeks, and then one day a very different woman came to see me. "The offered me the gig," she said in a tone which connoted foreshadowing more than completion, and I knew we would not be negotiating a typical compensation plan. "Actually I have two offers – one from the company that makes wines and ciders and vinegars, and the other from those people who do the fleece and down products. Both good money, more than I was making. They'd even give me an assistant with one of them," she said, her voice feeling flat to me.

"Why do I feel like we're not going to be talking about a bidding war for your services?" I smiled.

"Because I went for a walk in the trails out by the university last night – hours in the dark on the wet ground – and I know I just can't sell stuff anymore. Not even good stuff. Not even O list stuff. Not even organic or fair trade or cooperatively made stuff. I can't do it!" She paused, then… "You know I've been studying Qi Gong, right?"

"Yes, and vegetarian cooking and water colour painting, too, as I recall," I replied.

"Those and some meditation, bodywork modalities, even art therapy," Maureen added. "I used to find the damnedest ways to get them to approve my using my professional development funds for personal growth," she giggled. "My friends from Marketing school are all taking courses in positioning, web strategies, messaging, the Adobe suite, whatever, or applying to MBA programs, something big, always related to the work. I *love* classes and learning and I haven't taken one marketing-related class since I finished university. Why do you suppose that is?"

This was clearly a time when Maureen would answer that question herself so I just waited.

"I think I've already learned all I need to learn about that stuff. I don't think it was the point. It was more like laying groundwork for something. I know how to create challenge and excitement. I can take any project and grow it and make it personal and amazing. I did that all the way through school. I still do it in my courses now, always stretching, always flowing. When things feel good to me, it's like Qi Gong. Every movement stretches me gently and I extend myself into it, naturally, gracefully. I grow. I didn't do that in my old job. I sat there and stagnated. I didn't grow it and I didn't let it grow me. And I don't think that was just about the company anymore. I see it differently. I think I chose to close off because it was somehow the only way I could open in a different direction."

Maureen's voice was getting stronger and clearer as she spoke. "I *am* a communicator. I'm a synthesizer. I understand how to find a kernel and say it in a way that people get it. And I'm creative and I wanted to earn a good living to give me choices in life. So Marketing showed up as an obvious doorway. But just because it was my door doesn't mean it's my path. I just so completely *got* that last night when I was lost on the trails: it's time to stop circling around and trying to make this path satisfy. I'm done with that. I'm ready for a new road. So I need you to help me find a way to turn down these offers that won't cause too much hardship at their end, not make me look like a total flake on the job market, and then I need to take a few weeks to sort out my new direction. I'll use my marketing skills, but never in the same way again. I can't. I'm not the same person anymore," Maureen finished – as firm in her intention yet as soft in her presence as I had ever experienced her.

And by this time I was the one crying.

Maureen checked in periodically over the next few weeks but was in and out of town, staying with friends, visiting her parents, taking another class or two. She continued to email me bits and pieces of reflections along the way and as we cyber-dialogued I could start to see a pattern emerging in where she was being called: in fact, it was starting to look very familiar to me.

Her last email before leaving a friend's place on Vancouver Island to return to town for her next appointment said the following: "This may be kind of weird for you and I need you to know that I will understand if you don't think you can keep going with me on it and also to know that

> These are crucible experiences in life: what is true transforms into something more real; what is not true burns away.

I would never try to compete with you. I've been benefiting a lot from bodywork and art therapy and other very unique healing modalities most people have never even heard of and been struck by how much these gifted healers could use someone to help them clarify what they do and find their markets. So I think I want to use my branding and positioning skills to help healers position themselves, and to market themselves to their perfect clients, sort of like the work you do but maybe with more ad copy and consulting thrown in. I'd like to come in and talk to you about it at our meeting on Thursday but I wanted to put it out there ahead of time because this is so important to me, if you feel for any reason like you can't support it right now, then I need to go ahead on my own. Thank you for everything whatever you decide. You got me here and even if I have to take it the rest of the way myself or with someone else, I will forever be grateful for all you have done."

Maureen's beautiful voice brought tears to me yet again. I loved it most that she was so owning it, so committed to her vision that she would protect it from the world, even from me if that had been necessary. So beautiful to see. She was vulnerable, yes, but not scared. I emailed back only that I loved her news and couldn't wait to hug her... the rest we could share in person.

And so began the next wonderful phase: I mentor coached Maureen for a little over a year while she took some coaching and counselling courses, dabbled more in art therapy and explorations of mandalas, and read up on guerilla marketing strategies for micro-businesses. She very shortly found two communities of healing practitioners, who shared office space and referrals with one another, and who became her first clients, her practice growing right along with theirs. And in a very beautiful way, Maureen began looking more and more like herself every day.

That last part is a hard thing to explain to someone who has never experienced or witnessed it: all I can do it say you will know it when you see it. Authenticity and 'home-ness' have their own special radiant beauty. When people find that within themselves, it starts oozing out every pore. I hope you catch that light for yourself and bask in it when you can. I also hope you know that this bright light is always in you, even when you feel engulfed in darkness. Darkness is sometimes just blessing's disguise.

"I just got sandbagged by a power play on our Board and I've landed hard on my ass. Along the way I got a few kicks to the gut and head, too, and they made me realize I am so tired of being broke – it's a crappy way for a professional fundraiser to feel, and I want more. Out of everything. My friend says if anyone can help me over this hump, it's you." That's how Jerod described his state in our first conversation in which he outlined a sadly messy and passive-aggressive implosion of the organizational underpinnings of a major not-for-profit for which he had been the principal revenue engine for over a decade.

"More out of everything sounds like a pretty tall order, Jerod," I responded, "and I'm only half of this deal. But if you are willing to get clear on what you really want, where and how you want more, and you'll take every risk and be open to every learning, and you will choose to stop seeing barriers and see all the opportunities, *and* decide you are full-on ready for abundance, then, yes, I think we can do that together."

"Wow. That's a lot," Jerod mused.

"That's what more out of everything will look like. Sleep on it. Call me back in a few days. What you are describing is 'go big or go home' time, so check in and see if this is what you really want," I replied.

Jerod didn't call back. Several months went by, actually, and I had forgotten all about him. Then came a phone call from the former client, Ted, who had referred him in the first place. "You need to talk to Jerod again," he said. "The poor guy's whole world has crashed in and he needs you."

"I'd be happy to speak with any of your friends and see how I might serve," I responded, "but he's got to call me himself."

"I got him to agree to meet us both for lunch," Ted replied. "He doesn't want to come for a formal appointment but he'll meet you in person if I come with him and he can get a better feel."

I wasn't sure what this would be, but Ted had always shown himself to have both a good heart and sound judgment, so I agreed to meet the two of them the following week if Ted would assure me that we were, indeed, just having lunch and Jerod would get to choose what, if anything, he shared about what was going on for him. "No 'So we're here because Jerod needs X fixed.' He needs to find his own safety and his own voice," I said. Ted was unsure that Jerod would do choose to talk to me openly on his own, but I was clear with Ted that I would need him to be a compassionate matchmaker and witness but no more – Jerod and I wouldn't be able to really connect if he didn't choose it himself, and Ted came around.

Our lunch together arrived just a few days later, and was very pleasant: great salads, good stories of life and love, how these two had become friends, restaurants we enjoyed, movies we'd seen, and a couple of questions about how I got into this field and what I love about it. And then the cheque came. Ted gave me a hug and whispered "I'm sorry" into my ear just before Jerod shook my hand to go. I wasn't sorry. I knew it would be what it would be.

There was a message from Jerod on my voicemail by the time I got back to my office. He would like an appointment, please.

The handsome and composed man I had met at the restaurant overlooking the water was still very present when Jerod came to see me, but

> **Authenticity and 'home-ness' have their own special radiant beauty. When people find that within themselves, it starts oozing out every pore.**

he slowly drifted into soft focus as a much more raw and urgent version of self moved into foreground. The battle at Jerod's not-for-profit had taken many casualties: two of his former colleagues were on stress leave; two people had resigned from the Board; and he had been 'summarily fired' – though two lawyers had told him he had no wrongful dismissal case because the Board had given him several directives he had not followed. I gave him a referral to another very good lawyer who could take another pass at the evidence but told him I was not optimistic he would get a different response. Even if there were good reasons to have taken a different course than directed, the Board had created what looked to me like a solid liability shield. I further shared my view that most people turn their lives around faster by letting go of the fight over the past and focusing whole-heartedly on the future. It's not the path for everyone, but it's something to consider.

"Well, I've got enough lawyers in my life already," Jerod continued. "Just six weeks after I lost my job at the agency, I came home to find my wife packed to leave, the majority of the furniture already out of the house. She stayed to tell me she was divorcing me, but there was no conversation: she was gone! I was so freaked out by the whole thing, I went to drive to a friend's place – she had taken our bed and I wasn't about to sleep in the guest room. I was a mess, pretty shaken up. Never had anything like that happen... well, anyway, I cracked up the car that night. So now I'm Mr No-Job, No-Wife, No-Clue, House-up-for-Sale, Four-Times-a-Week-Chiro-and-Physio guy. How do you like that?"

"Not any better than you do," I assured him. "I don't like to see anyone in pain. I've had a few life crashes of my own, and certainly been through hundreds of them with clients I care about a great deal, and I feel for you. Really. That said, believing as I do that we create our own experiences – I'm sure Ted would have filled you in on that part, right?" Jerod nodded clearly, if not enthusiastically. "Okay, so believing that," I continued, "I am wondering if you are aware of any benefits for you out of this experience? Even if you wouldn't have chosen this to happen the way that it did, is there any part of you that wanted out of the job, out of the marriage, or to be taken care of... anything that might give more meaning to these events than just pain?"

Jerod reflected for a good three minutes before responding, "Okay, that marriage hadn't been good for awhile and I do know we're both better off apart. We might even be able to be friends now, and we really weren't friends anymore when we were together. And I suppose it's obvious I wasn't happy in that job, even before the political dramas started playing out. I wouldn't have left it now, not when the job market is so tough in the non-profit world, but I was getting sick of it. My job was to schmooze all the big donors and to get them to give their money to underwrite our big arts events. I just can't feel like I am making the world a better place by getting rich people to support ballet and opera that really only other levels of rich people appreciate, anyway," Jerod laughed ruefully – perhaps the first real smile I had seen from him.

"So, although the timing and the process kind of sucked, you can maybe see that it's a good thing that you got out of there?" I asked.

"A good thing? No," Jerod replied. "That's going a little far."

"Okay," I said. "What if you were to land a really great job, something you are totally happy in, and all the other puzzle pieces of your life fit together too, and then from that new place, you were to look back on this time. Do you think from there you could see it as a good thing?"

"Well, that's a big *if*," he said.

"Humour me. Play along – try to imagine it," I tried again.

"Yeah, okay, sure. Obviously if I were happier in some new place, I'd be glad to have gotten there, and however I got there would be a good thing. So if and when I ever get anyplace like that, I'll let you know," he conceded – sort of. He was kind of throwing down a gauntlet, too.

"You already did," I responded. "Now we need to get down to work."

Our process was initially slow: Jerod was going through so much, he had a habit of rescheduling appointments, completing only half of his homework, getting easily distracted, and coming back to me to ask me what we were doing and why we were doing it at regular intervals. When clients get scared, they also get very forgetful: they forget their confidence and competence; they forget how to get more than two things done in a day; they forget the things I tell them, even the ones they write down and we review. It's like their world feels so tenuous to them, they can't hold on to anything. But then they do. Hold on. Just a little bit at a time, and it builds.

So between physiotherapy, chiropractic, lawyer, mediator, realtor, mortgage broker, massage therapist, veterinarian and dentist appointments, Jerod managed to see me, clarify some of what he wanted for this next phase of his life, get a resume built, and start thinking about market research and networks. The personality metrics we had done suggested it would be important for him to be in a creative and fast-paced environment, where change was not merely managed but even sought. One of his great challenges in his previous role was battling the conservatism of the Board of Directors when he wanted to make bold moves that he thought would grow the organization and they responded by asking him to keep doing what they had always done – they didn't see anything broken and they were not open to his fixing. This tension led to one fight after another, and led me to invite Jerod to consider a world outside not-for-profits.

"What?!?" came his aghast first response. "But I've always worked for NGOs and charities. I've been fifteen years in the arts! I'm 42 years old – I can't change entire fields! There isn't time!"

I told him that I wasn't telling him to do it; I was asking him to consider how he felt about it… and now we know his first feeling is fear. I also said that the only thing harder than changing at 42 is changing at 52 or 62, and that the man who embraces change so well *in* his work could probably also, with enough encouragement, be persuaded to embrace a change *of* his work, too. And then we just let that one hang in the air: he could do with it what he would.

For the next few weeks, Jerod continued researching NGOs and arts agencies, mining his existing network and adding to it, doing lunch with a few of the key donors from the old days to see who or what they might know about organizations in transition and maybe needing a good change management person on their money team. All positive experiences… just nothing making either of us shout "Yes! That's it!" Once Jerod had sold his home and taken the immediate financial pressures away, we had engaged in several long discussions about his goals which had led us both to commit to each other that we wouldn't let him settle for anything less than that, so merely 'positive' wasn't good enough.

Then one day he said, very softly, "I think I met a big 'yes' a couple of weeks ago."

"Have you been holding out on me?" I asked.

"Apparently I've been holding out on *me*," Jerod replied. He looked scared for the first time in a long time, so I just held the space and waited for him.

"His name is Jim and he is a lawyer for an environmental defense fund kind of place. I don't actually completely know what they do, but it's good work if he's doing it," Jerod said, slowly, carefully – too carefully. Then he waited. And I waited, too. But he clearly wasn't going to talk.

"So Jim works for an environmental agency. Yet I'm somehow not feeling like you are looking to work for them, too," I observed.

"No," said Jerod. And waited again. For a full minute.

"Okay," I continued. "I'm glad it was a good meeting and you'll tell me the 'yes!' part when you're ready. Do you want to look over the postings you were going to pull from the job boards?"

"Sure," Jerod said, and brought out a whole bunch of postings. For Australian and American companies. Corporate project management and community consultation and stakeholder relations jobs – a long way from not-for-profit arts. And out of the country. Every one of them.

"We can do this two ways, Jerod," I said, as gently as I could. "I can pretend not to notice that all these jobs are in far away places and that they are all in new fields and we can just talk about the applications and interview prep, if that's what you need right now. Or, you can tell me why you are..."

"I'm gay," Jerod blurted.

"And Jim is?" I finished the thought.

"My first love," Jerod replied.

"Wow." I said. "And I'm guessing he's American or Australian?"

"Yes, Australian but working for an American outfit right now, coming to Vancouver every few weeks." Jerod says.

"And I'm sensing you feel like this relationship maybe has some legs?" I checked in.

"I really do," Jerod replied. And I could see he really believed it.

"Okay, then," I said. "This can go one of two ways: we can work on cross-border networking strategies now and you can dish with me about your cute boy and let me hug you later... or, I can hug you now, you can tell me all about him, and we can say screw the applications until next time. Your call."

Happily, hugging took priority.

Over the next few months, Jerod and I worked on his developing relationships with lots of Vancouver companies doing business in the US and Australia as a good avenue to open networks in those markets. The corporate work – since I'm sure you're wondering – came into focus once he became someone more open to change and risks. Jerod's frustration had been, as he called it, 'groveling for dollars' and not being in a position to see how it was spent. Turning the tables to be the person responsible for doling out the money and advising on or even setting criteria for how it would be used was a perfect turnabout. In this new kind of role he could choose to fund projects he felt were closer to his 'making the world a better place' goal; take more chances and move more quickly because the people managing the money in business generally get to set the pace; and he would earn more himself, in keeping with his newfound sense of abundance.

The only thing nagging at him was his sadness over needing to leave Vancouver in order to be with Jim. "Where does Jim want to live?" I asked. "He wants to live in Vancouver, too," came Jerod's reply. "He loves it here. But he has no visa. He can't work here. He has no job and no prospect of getting one."

"Jerod," I said, "I don't have high hopes for your getting a job in Australia." He looked shocked. "It's not that it can't be done – I've supported clients while they did it: Australia, England, Italy, all over Canada, the US, of course. It's just that they actually *wanted* to. I don't see you making this work if both of you want to be here. With everything you've been through now, don't you think it's time to go after what you really want? No more second choices?"

Jerod choked up a little before saying, "My life is so much richer now than I would ever have believed it could be before. So, yeah, I'm in. What do we do?"

"I'm not sure," I said, "but I know it starts with holding the vision. And then I'll make some calls."

We found a good immigration consultant for Jerod and Jim and she advised starting to look for a company that would sponsor Jim on a temporary work visa that could eventually be extended. So Jerod and Jim set about networking together on each of Jim's visits to the city. Then Jerod was offered a really good job with a major corporation: he'd be based in Vancouver (of course!), managing over $2M per year in charitable and community giving and overseeing sponsorship and relationships for 40 annual events around the whole of western Canada.

"If I take this job, I can't just up and move to Australia in a couple of months. If I accept, I am definitely staying here. And we have no plan for Jim yet. This is a big deal," Jerod said.

"That it is," I agreed. "It's also what you want, isn't it? Bad fear is telling you that you are in danger; good fear tells you when you are taking a risk toward what you want. Go big or go home, remember? Which is this?"

"I hate it when you do that," Jerod said.

"Yeah, I know."

Jerod took the job. But that's not the end of the story.

You're reading this in 2007 or later — I don't know what the laws will be in the future. But I worked with Jerod in 2003. Some of you will know already why that year is significant. For the rest, let me enlighten you: that summer, the provincial government of British Columbia, the westernmost Canadian province in which my home city of Vancouver is located, legalized gay marriage. So you know how Jerod's story worked out: marriage, immigration, two great jobs, and soon, I'm told, a child to make their family complete.

Make that three great jobs: mine counts, too!

One of the things about blessings that come to us in a package we might not have consciously chosen is that the healing process it takes to accept them as blessings — to feel the gratitude, and enjoy the new opportunities we create — brings a lot of love into our lives. From ourselves and from others. The shock, the pain, the intensity… all combine to help us get a little closer to being real. And not in the Dr. Phil way — though I am a fan of his 'defining moments and pivotal people' work and it's in line with what I mean. What fits for me more, though, is *The Velveteen Rabbit* way of being Real, brought home to me by my friend Gail Larsen, who runs a program called "Real Speaking" and reads these beautiful words at every retreat:

> "What is REAL?" asked the Rabbit one day, when they were lying side by side near the nursery fender, before Nana came to tidy the room. "Does it mean having things that buzz inside you and a stick-out handle?"
> "Real isn't how you are made," said the Skin Horse. "It's a thing that happens to you. When a child loves you for a long, long time, not just to play with but REALLY loves you, then you become Real."

"Does it hurt?" asked the Rabbit.

"Sometimes," said the Skin Horse, for he was always truthful. "When you are Real you don't mind being hurt."

"Does it happen all at once, like being wound up," he asked, "or bit by bit?"

"It doesn't happen all at once," said the Skin Horse. "You become. It takes a long time. That's why it doesn't often happen to people who break easily, or have sharp edges, or who have to be carefully kept. Generally, by the time you are Real, most of your fur has been loved off, and your eyes drop out and you get loose in the joints and very shabby. But these things don't matter at all, because once you are Real you can't be ugly, except to people who don't understand."

"Once you are Real, you can't become unreal again."

Blessings in disguise make us Real. I wish you enough of them to love all your fur off.

Afterword:

Beginning Again

I hope the stories on these pages have brought you some measure of recognition about your own career and life path: perhaps a resonant, warm or somewhat rueful snapshot of who you have been... a glimmer or flash of who you might like to become... and a few inspirations for how you can take your next steps forward.

I hope you have felt comforted by the realization that the highly talented and amazingly passionate people whose stories grace these pages have known confusion and fear just like yours, and they have thankfully also known great joy and celebration of love. I likewise would want you to feel called to a knowing of how you can best express yourself through purposeful and values-driven work/life, permission to step into your desires and manifest them fully, and an openness – equally idealistic and pragmatic – to the actions which will make your intention real.

My wish is for you to be able to look back on the time/importance hierarchy in the introduction and use the examples in the case studies throughout to locate yourself and create a plan for your moving up and down it: starting with visions and spirit, heading down through all the phases to demonstration of who you really are and then back up again, your action and experience informing your contemplative practice, cycling forward and expanding out, always growing.

My own philosophy of what makes a good book, particularly nonfiction in this genre, is that it gives me one idea, one reframe, one 'Aha' that I didn't have before. It is my greatest wish that I have brought you one such moment. For those of you who would like exercises to take your path further, a *Love Made Visible Workbook* is in the works and in the meantime I will post a few momentum-building do-it-yourself pieces *at www. alannafero.com.* I am at work on a blog for that site as well, and would love to have you post your own stories of clarifying values, finding purpose, creating self actualizing career opportunities and enjoying abundant rewards doing work you love. Questions and feedback may also be sent to lovereaders@alannafero.com.

At the end of the day, my message is a very simple equation: (1) seek to know yourself and to regularly update yourself on that knowing as you learn and grow + (1) act on that knowing in good faith with some practical knowledge of how job markets work = (2) your creating the self-actualizing reality of both a good life and a good living.

"Oh, please," I can hear a few of you saying, "It's not that easy." Ah, I reply, but I didn't say easy; I said *simple.* And simple is often hard to locate and harder still to stay focused on through life's ups and downs. In fact it can be very hard. But it's not complicated. Complicated is what we do to ourselves when we decide what we're facing is too hard so we deny ourselves the simple truth and cover it up with a bunch of rules, expectations, limiting beliefs, fears, dramas and other ways of getting in our own way. (Not, of course, that I personally would know… the intimacy of the prose already ensuring my cover is blown!) And under all of it is the simple truth that we all want to know who we are, to express that knowing in the world, and enjoy safety, sustenance, community, validation, growth and reward as we do so. Maslow's higher human values and peak experiences again.

It's the end of this book, and that marks the beginning of the next adventure.

When I was a young girl, I read as many as 20 books a week. My Dad took me to the library every two or three days as I burned through the five titles someone my age was allowed to check out at one time, a rule I hope they have now changed. As voraciously as I read, though, there were some books that I liked so much that I would "save" them. Having had the experience of loving a book so much that I was heartbroken when the story ended and there was no sequel, no solace, I began to learn early in a manuscript when I was getting that "attached" feeling and I would put myself on a page diet – half a chapter at a time before I had to switch books, to make it last. But if I really, really loved the book, I would wind up back to it after only a few pages of the surrogate title, anyway. I used to dream of a book that would never end, a series that, "Nancy Drew Does Infinity," would keep going, the characters growing up with me, the heroine always ready to inspire me to a new adventure.

I never found such a book in my youth… but I'm happy to say I've now written one as an adult. The pages may have reached the back cover of the manuscript, but the story is very much continuing. I am the heroine I always wanted to find at the centre of the story, living a life that is the plot I was so in love with I wanted it to go on and on. Getting here was not by any means a straight shot – the student and then teacher of literature that I have always been knew too much about the 'necessities' of build, narrative arc, complicating actions and consequences, twists and symbolism, and she wouldn't allow that to happen. I still have many ups and downs, and I'm probably too Italian and Scots-Irish, too Leo, too auburn-haired, to ever relinquish drama entirely, but I've landed in a good and loving place from which to write the next chapters.

I invite you to embrace your own journey, to write your own book with you as its heroic protagonist, and to please make your love visible in a work/life well lived.

About the Author
Alanna Fero, MA, LSC

Alanna Fero maintains a private practice in Vancouver, Canada, providing life purpose and business coaching, career management, executive leadership development, employee engagement consulting and recruitment services to local and international clients, working in person and via telephone, skype and email. In addition to the amazing individuals sampled in this book, Alanna proudly calls dozens of socially responsible and values-driven (triple and quadruple bottom line) companies among her clients, and takes great joy in supporting their leadership journeys and helping them to create workspaces where people love to come to play.

With more than seventeen years experience in teaching, facilitation, communications, career development, recruitment, executive coaching, employee engagement and workshop delivery, including a seven year tenure as a popular college professor; a two year stint as creator, executive producer and host of Canada's only recruitment radio show; and close to nine years in private coaching and consulting practice, Alanna loves leveraging the power of interpersonal relationships, provocative dialogue and good strategy to improve people's experience of their lives.

In addition to her practice, Alanna is a regular media commentator on subjects related to life purpose, career and business, and delivers keynotes and workshops on *Love Made Visible Work/Lives* to diverse audiences around North America. She is actively working on both a companion workbook to *Love Made Visible* and a study of top companies creating self-actualizing workplace cultures where love is just part of every workday.

Balancing her passion for supporting people to do good in the world and do well for themselves at the same time, in her spare time Alanna is fond of road trips, meditation and slow food.

www.alannafero.com

Love Made Visible
Keynotes and Workshops

From a one hour lunch n' learn or up to two hour keynote, and even half day, full day and multi-day interactive experiences customized to meet your organization's specific needs, **Alanna stands ready to deliver compelling programs that audiences and event planners remember fondly for years to come.**

Widely recognized as equally engaging, impactful and mindful to deliver high value ROI, the Love Made Visible™ experience as Alanna delivers it is tailor-made to elevate your audience while she is in the room and to send people off with takeaways you can easily integrate into your organization to improve energy, productivity, morale, team cohesion and employee retention.

Responses from past workshop participants:

- "I can't imagine anyone leaving one of Alanna's talks and not feeling lighter, more energized, better about themselves. Thanks!"

- "Alanna is understanding and very open to the concerns, attitudes and opinions of all the people in the room. She's a great facilitator and will go to any lengths to help people. Alanna is *real*."

- "Alanna really adapted to the changing needs of participants over the two days. She astounded me with her ability to go with the flow and still meet stated objectives. She's just a natural and holds space for learning so organically. As a presenter myself, I was in awe. Thank you for learning on many levels!"

- "She so clearly loves what she is doing. Never hits a false note. I'd enroll in anything with Alanna at the front of the room."

- "This woman knows what she's doing and knows how to get people moving."

- "Alanna is not just encouraging -- she's inspirational. I'd recommend her to anyone."

- "I understand what is important to me now like I never have before. I got so much more than I signed on for."

- "I can't imagine learning more or having more fun than we did today. Alanna rocks the house like no one else when passion and high energy are needed and she is gentle and easy when it's time to gear down. She adapts like nobody I've ever seen, and I've seen a lot. I look forward to next time."

Contact bookings@alannfero.com for details.

AWAKENING
AUDACITY
PEOPLE
POTLUCK
PARTY™

A LIFE LAUNCH LIKE NO OTHER!

ARE YOU READY TO
CELEBRATE YOUR LIFE?

IS IT TIME TO FOR YOUR
DREAMS TO TAKE CENTRE
STAGE?

HOW MUCH LIGHT
CAN YOU STAND?

Let Alanna and her team orchestrate an evening to launch you into your next adventure with all the inspiration, resources, structure and momentum you need to live the authentic and abundant life you've been dreaming about!

The Awakening Audacity™ experience combines the excitement of a stage show with the community spirit of a barn-raising and the powerful focus of the very best think tank.

...All the passion you feel on these pages ...brought to life for you, in person ...at a wildly creative and wonderful event planned and hosted for you and your friends (old and <u>new</u>!)

Visit alannafero.com for more details or contact audacity@alannafero.com to book your event.

(Tell your guests the food we'll have covered... just remember to bring a friend.)

ISBN 142513587-0

9 781425 135874